AAUG Monograph Series: No. 15

American Church Politics
and the
Middle East

Basheer K. Nijim, Editor

ASSOCIATION OF ARAB-AMERICAN UNIVERSITY GRADUATES, INC.
Belmont, Massachusetts 1982

ii

First published in the United States of America in 1982 by The
Association of Arab-American University Graduates

ISBN 0-937694-53-3

The Association of Arab-American University Graduates, Inc.,
was established in December 1967, incorporated as a non-profit
educational and cultural organization in the state of Michigan in
1968 and obtained tax-exempt status from the Internal Revenue
Service in 1970. The Association aims at promoting knowledge and
understanding of cultural, scientific and educational matters
between the Arab and American peoples. Membership is open to all
college graduates who are U.S. citizens or permanent residents and
who are of Arabic-speaking origin. Associate membership is open
to U.S. citizens or permanent residents interested in furthering the
aims of the AAUG.

For further information write to: AAUG, 556 Trapelo Road,
Belmont, MA 02178, 617-484-5483.

The editor gratefully acknowledges the invaluable
assistance of:

Sandra Heller, *Typing and Editorial Assistance*
Germana Nijim, *Editorial Assistance*
Sherijo Dullard, *Cartography*

Contributors

Rabbi Elmer Berger. President, American Jewish Alternatives to Zionism, Inc., Suite 404, 133 East 73rd St., New York, New York 10021.

Larry Ekin. Seminar Designer, United Methodist Office for the United Nations, 777 United Nations Plaza, New York, New York 10017.

Hassan S. Haddad. Professor of History, St. Xavier College, 103rd and Central Park Avenue, Chicago, Illinois 60655.

Beth E. Heusey. Staff of United Methodist Office for the United Nations and U.N. Representative for the Mennonite Central Committee, 777 United Nations Plaza, New York 10017.

Paul Jersild. Academic Dean, Wartburg Theological Seminary, 333 Wartburg Place, Dubuque, Iowa 52001.

Rev. Peter Johnson. Middle East Research & Information Project (MERIP), P.O. Box 3122, Washington, D. C. 20010.

Basheer K. Nijim. Professor and Head, Department of Geography, University of Northern Iowa, Cedar Falls, Iowa 50614.

Rev. Joseph L. Ryan. Rector, Jesuit Community, College of the Holy Cross, Worcester, Massachusetts 01610.

Contents

INTRODUCTION

Basheer K. Nijim

In no other international conflict is religion as pervasive a factor as it is in the Israeli-Palestinian conflict. This is so because of the profundity of the Judeo-Christian heritage which is manifested in an automatic association in the minds of millions of Americans and West Europeans between today's Israel and that of the Old Testament, in an obliteration of two thousand and more years of history, in the reiteration of the name Israel from Sunday pulpits, and in the widespread media empathy for Israel. It is uncommon to encounter a seriously articulated distinction between today's Israel and that of old and between Jews and Zionists, or to read an analysis of Zionism as a political movement with a sharply defined ethnic intention and territorial quest, or to see critiques of Zionism and Israel by thoughtful Jews and Christians concerned about justice and human rights. The specter of anti-Semitism has muffled many who have spoken out, many who do agree that the behavior of Zionism and Israel must be subjected to the same standards of analysis as the behavior of any other political action group or political institution. It has been the ill fortune of Palestinians to be the other party in the conflict involving Israel, and thus their plight has been largely unseen, or, worse, seen only through Biblical prophetic visors that have not only exacerbated their misery but made of their suffering a predestined happening, somehow divinely foreordained and sanctioned. To see the Deity as an adversary is awesome by any standard. If the conflict were between Palestinians and Greeks, or Palestinians and Ethiopians, or Palestinians and

Indonesians, it would never have received the attention that it has, to the consistent and devastating disadvantage of the Palestinians.

This book brings together incisive perspectives on these and related issues. Haddad's first paper (The Bible and the Question of Palestine: The Roots of Injustice) was first presented at a conference that addressed the subject Toward Biblical Foundations for a Just Peace in the Holy Land held in May 1981 in La Grange, Illinois. His second paper (Christian Zionism in America: The Religious Factor in American Middle East Policy) was originally presented at an Association of Arab-American University Graduates Symposium held in Beirut and hosted by the journal Shu'un Filastiniya in June 1979; it was published in Arabic in that journal, No. 92–93, July–August 1979, pp. 168–190). Nijim's paper is an expanded version of a presentation given at the annual meeting of the Association of American Geographers in 1978 in New Orleans. The other papers were all presented at the annual meetings of the Association of Arab-American University Graduates in 1979 in Washington, D.C., and in 1980 in Boston. As arranged here, the essays first consider the Biblical component of the Israeli-Palestinian conflict, then the nature of Zionism, and finally the positions taken by American church organizations on the conflict and the impact of the churches on American policy formulation. Church organizations, in addition to their spiritual role, are of major importance as educational and media institutions with an enormous influence on public opinion and policy formulation. It is this latter role that is examined in this volume.

In the opening paper on "The Bible and the Question of Palestine: The Roots of Injustice" Hassan S. Haddad notes that the quest for Biblical roots to the Israeli-Palestinian problem has sacralized the issue, and the result has been a polarizing of irreconcilable positions: if we make a connection between the state of Israel and Biblical Israel, then our search for principles of love and justice is in vain. Old Testament particularism excludes Palestinians from the scope of Biblical justice and charity towards the individual human being, and the Bible is used to justify behavior that otherwise cannot be morally justified. Instead of justifying or apologizing for Biblical particularism, we should honestly criticize it, for if injustice becomes of Biblical origin how may it be redressed by reference to the Bible? Also, when Biblical prediction is viewed as a form of predestination, humanity becomes in the service of a book instead of vice versa. Haddad observes that Biblical particularism is at least partly responsible for the Crusades, for imperial zeal, condescending Orientalism, Manifest Destiny, Apartheid, and for the tragedy of

Palestine. The challenge confronting those concerned about human rights in Palestine is to question and to put in moral perspective the Biblical idea of the covenant of chosenness. Haddad also notes that the Biblical attitude towards the "promised land" is the basis of Israel's policy of "land redemption," of dispossessing Palestinians. Jewish settlement becomes an act of piety. The final solution of the Canaanite problem, in terms of the covenant of damnation of the indigenous *goyim*, becomes a model for the final solution of the Palestinian problem. The land has to be *goyim rein*, whether Canaanite or Palestinian. Thus the Biblical destiny of Israel becomes incompatible with Biblical principles of love, morality, justice, and human rights. Palestinians become not only non-persons, but, together with Canaanites, anti-persons. Palestinians deserve not a covenant of peace through submission, but of total equality and justice. If at Auschwitz every Jew represented humanity, then, also, at Deir Yassin every Palestinian represented humanity. Otherwise all talk on the Israeli-Palestinian issue is futile rhetoric.

In the paper on "Biblical Zionism and Political Zionism" Basheer K. Nijim states that the term Zionism implies as a minimum an association between the Jewish people and a specific territory, an association embodied in a presumed covenant between Abraham and God. He compares the quest for land in Old Testament times with that in the twentieth century, that is by Biblical Zionism and Political Zionism. In terms of territorial extent both movements sought an area larger than that encompassed by Palestine. The term Eretz Israel (Land of Israel) as compared with the term the state of Israel is used by contemporary Zionists and Israelis to mean the "promised land," an area larger than that presently under Israeli control and occupation. Land acquisition in ancient times as in the present was by brutal conquest that occurred in stages over a period of time, with enclaves of territory that continued to be held and occupied by the indigenous inhabitants. Subjugation did not mean that peace followed. Zionism has always been explicitly exclusive. The people whose land was being conquered did not belong on their own land because they were not party to the covenant; they were not Jewish. Today the exclusivism is institutionalized in the state of Israel, notably in the Law of Return and in an anti-missionary law. The alleged divine right to land is atemporal: it starts retrospectively at the beginning of time and lasts forever. Its latest manifestation is the implanting of Jewish settlements on Palestinian Arab land in the West Bank and Gaza Strip. Nijim concludes by noting a contradiction between the land covenant with Abraham and the covenant with Moses that included the injunction "Thou shalt not covet," and he suggests that the prospects for peace would be enhanced if the Old Testament were regarded as the folk literature of a people.

In his paper "Zionism: Redemption or Retrogression?" Rabbi Elmer Berger observes that criticism of Zionism and of Israel has been inhibited by two misconceptions: that Zionism is rooted in the historic religion of Judaism, and that Zionism is a liberation movement. The values and ideology of Zionism are incompatible with Judaism, and it has been Zionist strategy to exploit Judaism to serve the end of Zionist statehood. Deception has been a modus operandi of Zionism, and Berger illustrates this trait by quoting from Zionist history. He points out that whereas Zionist leaders gained Jewish support especially because of Hitler, they were concerned that such support was merely for philanthropic concerns rather than in conscious support of the political objective of bringing about Jewish statehood. Berger condemns as guilty accomplices those Christian leaders who supported Zionism when they knew that pursuing and achieving the Zionist objective required usurping Palestinian rights and dehumanizing Palestinians. Even more guilty of moral irresponsibility have been America's political leaders. Opposition to Zionism has been branded as anti-Semitism, and Jewish critics of Zionism have not been immune to the harassment. Rabbi Berger then recounts specific cases of attacks on himself and on other anti-Zionist Jews by the Zionist establishment. He calls upon men of good will not to be inactive and reminds them of the necessity to "let the people know."

Writing on "Mainline Churches and United States Middle East Policy," the Reverend Peter Johnson observes that religion and politics are intimately related in the United States, despite the constitutional separation of church and state. His paper focuses on the "mainline Protestant denominations," namely Episcopal, Presbyterian, Congregational, and Methodist, plus the inter-church agencies that they dominate, because in general these are "the churches of the upper class." He briefly reviews the historic antinomy between Christians and Jews. When political Zionism emerged it was supported by some Christians because of the presumption of Biblical prophetic fulfillment and the related eventuality of the conversion of Jews. The first contacts of the mainline churches with peoples of the Middle East were in connection with missionary work early in the nineteenth century. Given the difficulty of the task, they soon diverted their energies to service, and many educational institutions were started. At the same time the attitude towards Arabs was one of moral and cultural superiority. Still, with the onset of Zionism it was these groups who were more understanding of the Arab position. They became involved in Palestine refugee relief as early as July 1948. A slight shift to a concern with political remedies, rather than engaging in merely humanitarian action, occurred at the 1956 conference of the World Council of Churches. Following the 1967 war the political nature of the "problem" became paramount, and a Palestinian community and identity were addressed: church work ought to be done *with* Palestinians and not *for* them. By the late 1970s the mainline churches were supporting Palestinian national aspirations, at least in some form. Rev. Johnson observes that the National Council of Churches has been consistently several years ahead of both the United States government and American public opinion in understanding Israel and the Palestinians and in advocating new approaches to the Arab-Israeli conflict. He concludes by noting the emergence of support for the Palestinian cause by some leaders of the American Black Christian community.

In his essay on "Theology and Politics in the Middle East: Some Christian Reflections," Dean Paul Jersild addresses the question of the meaning of the state of Israel in the light of scriptures. He notes that the question of land has always been important to the Old Testament faith, and one of his examples illustrating this religion-land association is an assertion by Moses Hess (19th century) that "it is the land that we lack in order to exercise our religion." Today most Israelis are not actively religious, yet the religious factor is prominent in Israel's claim to land. Christian criticism of Israel has been muted or totally suppressed by the fear of the label of anti-Semitism, an aspersion made, among others, by some Christian theologians who regard Israel as having a divine right to land. Jersild argues that much historical writing on this subject lacks historical sense by assuming a Biblical text to apply specifically to the time of the writer. He comments on the question of Biblical interpretation and argues that the need to reinterpret the scriptures, both Old and New Testaments, has been misused by Christians and Jews in asserting a twentieth century Israeli "right" to land and in prescribing solutions to contemporary international problems in the Middle East or anywhere else. He finds that Jewish liturgies and the Talmud give priority to people over land and to land over statehood, a distinction valid also from a Christian viewpoint. He challenges Israel to move beyond the Zionist mentality, and he concludes that "throughout Israel's history the *grasp* for land paradoxically brings the *loss* of land."

In the paper "Religion and United States Foreign Policy Towards the Middle East: A Catholic Perspective" the Reverend Joseph L. Ryan focuses on official documents on the Middle East issued by United States Catholic bishops from 1973 to 1978. There is a consistent support for Israel expressed in statements directed to the United States public, American Catholics, the Christian church, inhabitants of the Holy Land, people of Lebanon, Palestinians, the United Nations, President Carter, the United States, and even to the Soviet Union. Not once is Israel called upon to act in a particular way. Rev. Ryan makes the point that churches are not only major structures in the United States, but major media as well. The Roman Catholic "ministry of justice" has great potential strength, is open, and is likely to be increasingly active. He then briefly considers how institutional Catholicism in the United States comes to its policy decisions, what results the process brings about, and what the future prospects are. Too often statements of official leaders have not dealt with the inherent merits of issues because of an overriding concern for the ecumenical problem, for instance supporting Israel for the sake of improved relations with American Jewish groups. The trend now is towards addressing issues involving justice, and among these is the disinheriting of Palestinians whose inclusion as independent participants in any negotiations on the Middle East problem is both politically sound and morally necessary.

In Hassan S. Haddad's second paper in this volume, "Christian Zionism in America: The Religious Factor in American Middle East Policy," the major hypothesis is that the pro-Israel anti-Arab sentiment of the American public is primarily the product of a religious conviction and is not based on reasoned economic or political considerations or on knowledge of international politics. The term Christian Zionism refers to the Biblically oriented Christian support of Israel and is found among Presbyterians, Lutherans, Episcopalians, and Catholics, as well as fundamentalist Protestants, all of whom have engaged in wide-ranging pro-Israel propaganda, whether from pulpits and Sunday schools or through published material. Haddad surveys tortuous theological statements by Christian Zionists, statements that appear to abandon the principle of individual justice, and then relates the activism of the Christian Council on Palestinian in concert with American Zionist leaders. Support for Israel immediately following its establishment in 1948 was tied to an obsession with anti-communism and a feared Soviet involvement in the Middle East. The 1967 war led to greatly increased millennial interpretations of the conflict in the Middle East, and support for Israel was presented by some as a commitment of faith: military and other support conforms with and hastens the Second Coming of Christ, and opposition to Israel must be anti-Christian and against God. This eschatalogical perspective was greatly popularized in books, magazines, movies, radio, and television. The 1970s witnessed an increase in evangelical influence, with a concomitant increase in grassroot support for Israel, a support that was and continues to be politically active. To call the Jewish state formed in 1948 "Israel" was to score an immediate and enormous public relations coup.

In the paper on "The New Christian Right and Zionism" Larry Ekin points out that fundamentalists and born-again Christians comprise about a third of the American population. The many groups that fall into this category agree on such matters as interpreting the Bible literally, regarding the Bible as scientific as well as theological truth, opposing the teaching of evolution, opposing the Equal Rights Amendment, opposing abortion, attacking pornography, supporting public school prayer, and supporting Israel. Whereas these positions are not new and are shared by non-fundamentalists, what is new and significant is the politicization of these concerns and the concerted political activism of the various groups. Ekin illustrates the confluence of right-wing politics and the evangelical movement by describing the Religious Round Table which brings together leaders of such organizations as the National Christian Action Coalition, the Moral Majority, the Christian Voice, Campus Crusade for Christ, and the Christian Broadcasting Network. Their support of Israel is based on a theological interpretation of the Bible. In Jerusalem in September 1980 an "International Christian Embassy" was established which acts as if it were an agency for Israel and Israeli commercial products. The Israeli government has been quick to capitalize on this support, illustrated for instance by an urgent phone call from Menachem Begin to Jerry Falwell asking him to explain to the Christian public the reasons for Israel's bombing of the Iraqi nuclear reactor. The activism of the New Right groups will continue to manifest itself in United States political elections.

The concluding paper by Beth E. Heisey addresses the subject of "Impacting United States Church Policies on the Middle East." Heisey states that if Arab-Americans wish to communicate with church leadership in the United States or to have an impact on the formulation of Middle Eastern policy they must address the church in a comprehensive and systematic manner. The strength of the organized church stems from membership numbers, economic power, a far-reaching economic structure, an educational role, and

an image as a moral and spiritual force. Christianity's Jewish roots
are especially significant in connection with Middle Eastern issues.
Church policies take the form of policy statements or resolutions,
for instance the statement passed in November 1980 by the National
Council of Churches of Christ/U.S.A. Such statements should be
taken seriously, even though there is a considerable gap between
the church leadership and the average church-goer. Heisey then
enumerates specific steps that can be taken at the grassroots level
to help explain realities of the conflict in the Middle East.

1

The Bible and the Question of Palestine:
The Roots of Injustice

Hassan S. Haddad

The task of finding Biblical foundations for a just peace in the Holy Land is a formidable one because the problem of Palestine has firm Biblical roots. It should not be difficult to find Biblical texts promoting justice and peace; but what makes the task difficult, and what has made it so far unattainable, is the fact that this issue has been sacralized, or biblicized. It is as if the case for Palestine and for Palestinian human rights has been prejudiced already by its Biblical nature. Upon some reflection on the holiness and the turbulent history of this unhappy land one can see that the Bible and the Biblical view shared by Christians and Jews is primarily responsible for its plight.

The search for Biblical foundations for justice and peace in the Holy Land has to face the initial hurdle of deciding why the injustice occurred in the first place and to look into the Biblical foundations of that injustice. If we accept the link between modern Israel and Biblical Israel, the search for justice for the Palestinian people will remain in vain. The question is not whether there are Biblical texts recommending love, justice and brotherhood, but whether these statements can withstand the greater impact of other Biblical texts promoting the doctrine of the centrality to human destiny of Israel as *Chosen People* and a *particular state* in a *Promised Land*.

Biblical Quotations are taken from *The New English Bible*, New York: Oxford University Press and Cambridge University Press, 1970.

It is not difficult to find texts promoting love of neighbor and good behavior toward the foreigner. But can it be established, without going against the Biblical thrust, that these good commandments have the priority over the concept of chosenness, of election according to birth, or the doctrine of the covenant? Based on the teaching of Jesus, the answer should be clear. Jesus put love of God and love of neighbor above all commandments. The question that was then put to him "who is my neighbor?" symbolized Biblical particularism which was prevalent at the time of Jesus as it is today. The parable of the Good Samaritan cleared the riddle of neighbor. Jesus leaves no doubt that the covenant doctrine does not determine who the neighbor is, and that love and human consideration are not bound to chosenness, religious affiliation, or faith. (Luke 10:25-37).

However, when confronted with the question of Palestine and of Palestinian human rights, most people are intimidated by the Bible. There are those who are convinced that the Bible gives nothing to the Palestinians for opposing Israel, because they are convinced that the Bible makes a total commitment to give the land of Palestine to the Jews. There are those who feel pity for the dispossessed and the refugees, but refuse to go further in their support fearing contradicting the Bible. And those who think that two rights are in conflict over Palestine are torn between their sense of justice and charity towards the individual human being regardless of birth or affiliation, and their belief in the particular privilege conferred collectively on the seed of Jacob.

The important point is this: to find justice in the Bible is not impossible nor difficult. The quest for Biblical justice is controverted because Israel is the central theme of the Old Testament and is very much the concern of the New. This draws a picture of particularism, of favoritism, and discrimination. To let this go unchallenged, to try to go around this particularism, to apologize rather than honestly criticize, will only exacerbate the plight and suffering of innocent people.

We should be aware of the pitfalls of seeking the Biblical road to redress injustices which can be attributed to Biblical origins. Bibliolatry, which is becoming more rampant, puts humanity in the service of the book, not the book in the service of humanity. The Bible should be studied from the perspective of history. We have seen how, too often, history has been viewed in the West only from a Biblical perspective. Western acceptance of the idea of the Jewish State in Palestine and practical support of Israel is motivated by the Biblical world-view.

Another pitfall is the typological interpretation of the Bible. This sees Old Testament events as prefiguring New Testament ones, and by extension modern and current events. People have sought and found Biblical models —meaning justifications—for their behavior, especially the type of behavior that cannot be justified on grounds of human morality and fairness.

Biblical predictive prophecy is another pitfall that is taking serious proportions. While Biblical history is used to provide justification for greed, self-centered attitudes, and deprecation of others, this bias is projected into the future because prophetic texts in the Bible did so. It is claimed, therefore, that the goal of history is centered on a particular tribe, nation, or church—all this, of course, is predicated on the centrality of Israel—by divine design.

Between a Biblical restrictive history and a Biblical predictive prophecy human rights are lost in what is called a divine right claimed by one party to the exclusion of all others.

This Biblical view has been responsible in whole or in part for the Crusades and the pervading crusading spirit, for the discriminatory attitudes of colonialists, missionaries, and orientalists, for America's Manifest Destiny and South Africa's apartheid, and, of course, for the tragedy of Palestine.

It is easy to be aware, even after an elementary study of American history, of the devastating effect of the concept of manifest destiny—the idea that America is the new Israel—on the Indians, the African slaves, and the less fortunate neighbors of the Anglo-Saxon commonwealth. Robert Bellah in *The Broken Covenant* puts it very aptly:

> Thus at the very beginning of American society there was the primal crime against the Indians. . . . For a long time, indeed for centuries, the new settlers failed to appreciate the fact that the people they found here lived in a different dream. Whether the Indian was seen as noble or as horrid savage, he was treated as if he were a character in the European dream, as if he had no dream of his own. . . . This failure to see the Indians in their own terms was only the cultural side of a denial of humanity that was also expressed in economic and even biological terms. The Indians were deprived by the new settlers, not only of the inherent human right to have one's culture understood and respected, but they were ruthlessly deprived of land and livelihood and all too often of life itself. This was the primal crime on which American society is based. . . . We must ask what in the dream of White America kept so many for so long, so many even at this day, from seeing any crime at all. For that we need to consider the ambiguities of chosenness.[1]

Substitute the terms America and Indians with the terms Israel and Palestinians to realize how much the Biblical concept of chosenness, of covenant, is responsible in both cases for the primal crime. It is clear that the justification of this primal crime, or at least its veiling in a shroud of respectability, lies squarely at the door of the doctrine of covenant. The prototype of chosen White America (and of modern Israel) is Biblical Israel. And the *figura* of the despised and dispossessed Indian (and of the modern Palestinian) is also Biblical: the Canaanites, the *indigenous goyim*. They were also cynically chosen to bear the eternal curse that explains and justifies the primal crime.

The totally uncompromising attitude toward the Canaanites finds a mythical origin in the book of Genesis. The story goes that Canaan, father of the Canaanites, received an eternal curse upon his person and his descendants, because of something his father, Ham, did. Ham, according to the Biblical legend, happened to see his own father, Noah, naked and drunk and made fun of him. Noah, after sobering up, delivers a curse and a blessing: "Cursed be Canaan, slave of slaves shall he be to his brothers," and he continued: "Bless O Lord, the tents of Shem; may Canaan be his slave." (Genesis 9:25, 26)

The legend sets the stage for the conquest of the land of Canaan by the descendants of Shem, the Israelites. Ham, the one who sinned, was not cursed because, as rabbinical interpretations maintain, he had already received the blessing of God bestowed on Noah and his sons.

The American example of chosenness is, at best, a mirror image of Biblical Israel. But modern Israel is claimed as the direct descendant of the Biblical one, a continuation and fulfillment of a historical fact based on a divine election and a sacred promise of land. While Zionist thinkers also attempt to present Jewish nationalism as a modern movement based on conditions present in the nineteenth and twentieth centuries, the fact remains that, ideologically, ethnically, and territorially this modern movement is primarily based on Biblical Israel. The name "Zion" focuses on the territorial definition of Israel in the Bible. The name "Israel" reflects the intertwining of racial and territorial considerations found in the Bible, in traditional Jewish beliefs, and in rabbinical literature. Consequently, when Zionists speak of their historic right to Palestine, they refer to a history and to a historical philosophy found in the Bible and the rabbinical literature. To deny the "historic right" of the Jews to Palestine is to challenge the scriptures. This is an article of faith to some Jews and Christians, but it also becomes a very effective public relations tool to influence the Christian world favorably towards Israel.

Accordingly, settling in Palestine, in addition to its economic and political motivations, acquires a romantic and mythical character for Zionist Jews. That the Bible is at the root of Zionism is recognized by religious, secular, non-observant and agnostic Zionists. Thus Moses Hess, who preceded Herzl and who is considered one of the fathers of the Zionist philosophy, recognized and preached the principles of interdependence of religion and nationalism in Jewish life. To him Jewish religion was, above all, Jewish nationalism; and both have firm Biblical foundations.[2] Ben Gurion was often Biblical in his writings and speeches, calling the Bible the "sacrosanct title-deed to Palestine" for the Jewish people "with a genealogy of 3500 years."[3] Dr. Jacob Talmon of the Hebrew University states that "the Jews are a community of fate, the product of history crystallized round the nucleus of race and religion."[4]

The Biblical spirit of exclusivism was well expressed by Ben Gurion when, addressing an international conference, he declared that "the Jewish vision of redemption has two aspects: the ingathering of exiles and the continuation of the Jewish people in its land as a chosen people, and as light to the nations."[5]

The Biblical concepts of promise, choice and the covenant are supra-rational, sacralized concepts producing a sacred historical right exclusively for the Jews and exclusively in Palestine. Justice and conventional human rights are merely of mundane and profane nature. The conquest of Canaan under Moses and Joshua, the attempt of Ezra and Nehemiah to establish a Jewish commonwealth within the Persian Empire, and the current Zionist colonization of Palestine all fall in this category of supra-rational action sacralized beyond normal legal and moral considerations. Zionists may or may not be practicing religious Jews, but a Biblical attitude toward the state, the land and the people, of who owns and who is disenfranchised from ownership of the land, has permeated their thinking and their action. A similar attitude toward the problem of Palestine is found among many Christians because of their Biblical background.

This is then the challenge in confronting the question of human rights for the Palestinians: to question and to put in moral perspective this basic Biblical idea of covenant and chosenness. We have been bold in challenging the applicability of this concept to American society. We are often daring in rejecting the claims of the Afrikaans to the covenant on moral and humanistic grounds. But we have been intimidated by the Biblical form and content of the

Jewish state. This Biblical connection of modern Israel, if accepted without challenge, will limit greatly the search for expressions of justice and equality in the Bible and will put a damper on the quest for human rights of the dispossessed Palestinians.

The concept of Promised Land is tied closely to that of chosenness, further strengthening the current of Israeli particularism and intransigence. Without the land, the covenant would have no earthly basis and an important part of the Torah and the Prophets would lose relevance. Rabbi Wolfe Kelman, Chief executive officer of the International Association of Conservative Rabbis, commenting on a proposed Vatican document concerning Judaism, welcomed in particular the document's "recognition of the reality of the State of Israel," its assertion that Jewish fidelity to the Old Covenant between God and the people of Israel is "linked to the gift of land, which, in the Jewish soul, has endured as the object of aspirations that Christians should strive to understand and respect."[6]

Rabbi Nissim, Chief Rabbi of Israel in 1968, made the following statement:

> The Land of Israel was, with its borders, defined for us by Divine Providence. Thou shalt be, says the Almighty, and there it is; no power on earth can alter that which was created by Him. In this connection it is not a question of law or logic: neither is it a matter of human treatment or that sort of thing.[7]

This Biblical attitude towards the Promised Land is behind Israel's policy of "land redemption," of dispossessing Palestinians and restricting ownership and development of property to non-Jews, of the constitution of the Jewish National Fund, and of the settlement policy in "Judaea and Samaria."

In view of this attitude toward the land of Palestine, settlement in it becomes an act of piety, righteousness, and religious duty for Jews. The covenant, or the concept of divine chosenness and promise applied to the land of Palestine, is one of the formidable obstacles in the road to peace and justice in the "Holy Land."

There is another side to the covenant which is closely related to the denial of human rights to the Palestinians. It is what I call the *negative covenant*, or the covenant of damnation which the Bible confers on the Canaanites, the *indigenous goyim*. The extermination, dispossession, dispersion and boycott of the indigenous population of Palestine which the Biblical text makes clearly imperative is at the roots of Israel's treatment of the indigenous

Palestinians. The final solution of the Canaanite problem in Biblical time stands as the *figura* for the final solution of the problem of the Palestinians in modern times.

The Bible seems to make the destiny of Israel and that of the Palestinians mutually exclusive. Just as the American Indian had to be removed to make room for the White American, the removal of the Palestinians is now a *sine qua non* for the purity, welfare, and security of the Jewish State. One party had to disappear to make room for the other, not because they *could not*, but because they *should not* live together. The Biblical injunction on mixing of the two races, on cultural pluralism, is quite clear and it applies to both cases.

The texts of the Torah and the historical books (especially Ezra and Nehemiah) advance the claim of ownership to Palestine as an absolute right of the Jews, not subject to the historical title of the Palestinians, to international law which supports this title, or to the basic humanitarianism that should have prevented the exile of the Palestinians. In practice, modern Israel seems to have wholly adopted the Biblical blessing and the Biblical curse: the blessing exclusively reserved for the "holy race," the "chosen people," and the curse, placed in eternity on the indigenous *goyim*, be they called Canaanites or Palestinians.

Seizure of the property of the Palestinians is demonstrably based on arbitrary choice of race sanctioned by Biblical precedence. It is not based on right, legal or moral, but on a supra-rational entitlement of one party and a mysterious disenfranchisement of another. Deuteronomy 6:10 makes this quite clear:

> The Lord your God will bring you into the land which he swore to your forefathers Abraham, Isaac and Jacob that he would give you, a land of great and fine cities which you did not build, houses full of good things which you did not provide, rock-hewn cisterns which you did not hew, and vineyards and olive trees which you did not plant.

The greatest measure of Biblical wrath and fury is directed not against those who enslaved, captured, or exiled the Chosen People, but against the original inhabitants of the Promised Land, be they Canaanites, Jebusites, Hittites, or any other dwellers on the land. The Bible argues not only that the political structure of the Israelites could possibly be threatened by the existence of the Canaanites, but that the cultural and religious character of Israel would be undermined by their continued presence:

You must not make a treaty with them or spare them. You must not intermarry with them, neither giving your daughters to their sons, nor taking their daughters for your sons; if you do, they will draw your sons away from the Lord and make them worship other gods. Then the Lord will be angry with you and will destroy you quickly. But this is what you must do to them; pull down their altars, break their sacred pillars, hack down their sacred poles and destroy their idols by fire, for you are a people holy to the Lord your God; the Lord your God chose you out of all nations on earth to be his special possession. (Deuteronomy 7:1–6).

The example of the conquest of Jericho, as we read in the book of Joshua, reveals a cruelty that was to be a recommended policy in dealing with the conquered towns of Canaan: "Everything in it belongs to the Lord, no one is to be spared." The Israelites thus destroyed everything in the city; they put everyone to the sword, men, women, young and old, and also cattle, sheep and asses (Josh. 6:17, 18, 21). Many more examples of extreme measures bordering on genocide can be cited.

The restrictive laws of modern Israel concerning marriage, cultural exchange, and education reflect the bias of the Biblical text. Socially, politically and economically, the segregation and inequality imposed upon the Arabs in Israel today demonstrate the continuity of a spirit of Biblical exclusivism.

The Biblical destiny of Israel is closely linked with that of the land and with the fate of the *indigenous goyim*. The land has to be *goyim rein*, free from the Canaanites, the Palestinians, in order to be consecrated to the Lord. The destiny of Israel depends on the eradication of the Canaanites. Thus the Biblical destiny of Israel is incompatible with Biblical morality. The question arises: which is more important?

In 1899, David Starr Jordan, President of Stanford, wrote that if "the Anglo-Saxon has a destiny incompatible with morality and which cannot be carried out in peace, if he is bound by no pledges and must ride rough shod over the rights and wills of weaker peoples, the sooner he is exterminated the better for the world."[8] Jordan stumbles at the end of the statement into the trap of excessive solutions. But he draws our attention to the incompatibility of the destiny of the new Israel with morality, and to the fact that such destiny thrives on war and discrimination.

It is also quite important to note that this incompatibility does exist today as it did in the Biblical prototype of the people of destiny. Biblical texts leave no doubt that Israel was ordered by the Lord to kill and disperse the Canaanites and the rest of the original inhabitants of Palestine. Even the Lord did his great share. The early books are saturated with the blood of the nations. Their guilt was uniform: they did not think they should leave, they had a different dream, and they did not belong to the right race. In short, they were not entitled to have human rights.

The fury of the ancient history of Israel pales in comparison with its Biblical apocalyptic destiny. The Canaanite holocaust is but a miniature example of the final holocaust to come at the fulfillment of history, when Israel will be firmly established by divine mandate to dominate all the nations, but not until the Lord will have turned the planet into a gigantic crematorium which will consume most of humanity.

This gaping gulf between the historical and political conceptions of the Bible and its moral code is difficult to bridge. It calls for a commitment to humanistic moral precepts on which total agreement is not impossible. It also calls for shelving or discarding the more enigmatic, more controversial typological interpretations dealing with origins and eschatology and saturated with particularism. A decision should be made to the effect that if the covenant did not agree with moral precepts and could not be carried out peacefully, the covenant loses. We should hold to this position as a pre-condition to any attempt to find Biblical foundations on which to build peace and brotherhood in the Middle East. That the covenant should be subject to the principles of love, equality, and human rights is a rule that should be applied to a judgment on the American Manifest Destiny, on South Africa's apartheid system, and on Israel's Zionist philosophy and practices. That these principles of love, equality, and human rights are at the essential core of the Biblical message does not appear to be contested here. There only remains the task of affirming priorities, and applying Biblical moral sanctions to Biblical excesses. This does not seem to be an easy task.

Reinhold Niebuhr is probably the most pominent modern American theologian. His total support of Israel was based on theological deliberations and some feeling of guilt caused by Nazi persecution of the Jews. His sense of justice and his Christian compassion, however, made him sensitive to the plight of the Palestinian Arabs. He therefore recommended that they be well-treated, compensated, and settled somewhere else other than in Palestine, their original home. Niebuhr's sense of justice was restricted by his theology. His discrimination between what is right for Jews and what is right for non-Jews was caused by his attachment to the doctrine of the covenant with its two dimensions of Chosen People and Promised Land. Recourse to this fundamental Biblical doctrine makes it possible, it seems to me, to preach total equality anywhere in the world except in the Holy Land.

Martin Buber's humanistic theology led to the same blind alley. His *Brit Shalom* was sincerely conceived to allay the fears of the Arabs in Palestine and to preach peace and tolerance. But his complete insistence on the eternal relevance of the Biblical covenant and of the chosenness of Israel controverted the universal aspect of humanism. Examples of Martin Buber's Zionist views, especially his theology of land, can be found in his *On Zion: The History of an Idea* (Schocken Books, New York, 1973). See also Martin Buber, *Israel and the World: Essays in a Time of Crisis* (Schocken Books, New York, 1948). Of special interest to the reader may be his article in this work entitled "The Land and Its Possessors" which is Buber's response to Gandhi's criticism of Zionist colonialism in Palestine. The open letter was written in 1939. The Arabs of Palestine deserve more than a covenant of peace, which could be obtained through submission. They need and deserve a covenant of total equality and total justice.

It is easier to understand, but not appreciate, the attitude of people like Rabbi Meir Kahane who do not equivocate. Kahane thinks that Torah Judaism demands that Israel should be free as soon as possible from Arabs. He asks, with pertinence, how can we have a Jewish state and risk having an Arab majority.[9] If the exclusive covenant is relevant to Israel, then the denial of total rights to the Palestinians becomes a necessity justifiable on Biblical grounds.

An article in *Christianity and Crisis* by Tom Driver has an interesting title: "Hating Jews for Jesus' Sake."[10] In it Driver deplores the fact that Christianity has carried in its soul something that he calls "the latent doctrine of the nonperson." "That is, there is a tendency in Christianity to regard all persons who do not conform to the model of Christ as less than full persons. . . . Their prayers are not heard. Their freedom does not matter."[11]

It is essential to recognize that the doctrine of the nonperson is a product of the doctrine of the favored person. And while Christianity bases the distinction between the favored and the disfavored on the acceptance of Christ, the old Biblical doctrine of covenant makes it a condition of birth. More than that, this doctrine introduces another category of discrimination: Gentiles may be nonpersons according to this doctrine, but the Canaanites, the indigenous goyim, the Palestinians, are *anti-persons*.

Rehabilitation of the Palestinian anti-person thus becomes more difficult. It has a longer road to travel, a road blocked by Biblical, theological and cultural hurdles. We cannot with clear conscience subscribe to half-measure solutions because of Biblical restrictions. We must not rehabilitate the Palestinians by extending the racial scope of the covenant, by claiming Abrahamic descent through Ishmael. And we cannot buy back a belated blessing on the Palestinians with another pottage of lentils.[12]

Emil Fackenheim wrote in the *Christian Century* (May 6, 1970): "At Auschwitz every Jew represented all humanity when for reasons of birth alone he was denied life . . ."[13] This is a true and revealing statement. But if we cannot substitute the word Jew with the word Indian, African, or Arab, we would be falling again in the trap of particularism. And if we cannot substitute Auschwitz with Deir Yassin because of the restrictive influence of the Biblical doctrine of the covenant, then all we would accomplish here would be futile rhetoric. For "I may speak in tongues of men or of angles, but if I am without love (unrestricted by particularism), I am a sounding gong or a clanging cymbal."[14]

NOTES

1. Robert Bellah, *The Broken Covenant*, New York: The Seabury Press, 1975, pp. 36–37.
2. Moses Hess, *Rom and Jerusalem: A Study in Jewish Nationalism*, translator Meyer Waxman, New York: Bloch Publishing Co., 1943.
3. David Ben-Gurion, *The Rebirth and Destiny of Israel*, New York: Philosophical Library, 1954, p. 100.
4. Norman Bentwich, "Judaism in Israel," in *Religion in the Middle East*, A. J. Arberry, editor, Vol. 1, Cambridge: Cambridge University Press, 1969, p. 76.
5. David Ben-Gurion, *Ben-Gurion Looks at the Bible*, translated by J. Kolatch, New York: Jonathan David, 1972, p. 111.
6. Wolfe Kelman, *Christian Century*, January 14, 1970, p. 39.
7. *Hayom*, June 7, 1968.
8. Quoted in Bellah, op. cit., p. 60.
9. See Meir Kahane's statement in the Readers' Letters, *Jerulsalem Post*, August 3, 1980, quoted from *Journal of Palestine Studies*, Vol. X, No. 1, Autumn 1980, pp. 152-153. (In this source the writer's name is spelled Kahana. Kahane is used here to conform with published works by him in English.)
10. Tom F. Driver, "Hating Jews for Jesus' Sake," *Christianity and Crisis*,

November 24, 1980, p. 325 ff.

11. *Ibid.*, p. 335.

12. This is a reference to the biblical story of how Jacob, although not the first born of Isaac, managed to get the blessing and to inherit the promise, bought for his brother Esau, with a pottage of lentils. Genesis 2.

13. Emil L. Fackenheim, *Christian Century*, May 6, 1970.

14. I Corinthians 13:1.

2

Biblical Zionism and Political Zionism

Basheer K. Nijim

What is Zionism? Whereas answers to this question may vary in
matters of detail, in all cases there will be a clear association
between the Jewish people and a specific territory. The *Jewish
Encyclopedia*, printed in 1925 and thus written barely a couple of
decades after the convening in 1897 of the first Zionist Congress,
defines Zionism as a "Movement looking toward the segregation of
the Jewish people upon a national basis and in a particular home of
its own."[1] The more recent *Encyclopaedia Judaica* (1971) refers to
the term Zion, the root of the word Zionism, as having had "a special
meaning as far back as after the destruction of the First Temple in
expressing the yearning of the Jewish people for its homeland."[2]
This people-land association is specific in terms of both of its
components: the people are the Jewish people, and the land is the
"promised land," the Land of Israel. In Old Testament times this
association was embodied in a Covenant with God, a Covenant that,
according to the *Jewish Encyclopedia*, was meant "to perpetuate
the three possessions: the land, the Davidic monarchy, and the
Aaronitic priesthood."[3] According to the *Encyclopaedia Judaica*
three covenants were concluded: with Moses (in the book of Exodus
and Deuteronomy), with Abraham (Genesis chapters 15 and 17),
and with David (II Samuel chapter 7). The covenant with Abraham is
the one that concerned the gift of land: "God swears to Abraham to
give the land to his descendants."[4] God's oath to Abraham is
recorded in Genesis 26:3. God is speaking to Abraham's son, Isaac:

"Stay in this country and I will be with you and bless you, for to you and to your descendants I will give all these lands. Thus shall I fulfil the oath which I swore to your father Abraham."[5] God's oath is also referred to in Deuteronomy 1:8. Here Moses is addressing his followers and quotes God as having said: "I have laid the land open before you; go in and occupy it, the land which the Lord swore to give your forefathers Abraham, Isaac and Jacob, and to their descendants after them."

I am not a theologian, and so I do not delve into exegesis. I do know that learned and brilliant theologians disagree on a whole range of Biblical interpretation, and I do not know who is right. As a political geographer my interest is in the behavior of people to the extent that that behavior has relevance to land and resources and to attendant competition and conflict, as well as cooperation and conflict resolution. Thus I become very interested in the religious belief and interpretation of a particular decision-maker, irrespective of whether or not I agree with the belief and with the interpretation. My purpose here is to look at the quest for land in Old Testament times, that is Biblical Zionism, and to compare it with twentieth century political Zionism. I will do so under four headings: territorial extent, land acquisition, exclusivism, and divine right and holy war.

1. TERRITORIAL EXTENT

Old Testament definitions of the "promised land" vary according to the time they were made, to whom they were made, and to the general situation of the Jews at the respective times. Three categories of territorial description can be identified.[6] One was to the Patriarchs, for instance in Genesis 15: 18-21.

> That very day the Lord made a covenant with Abraham, and he said, 'To your descendants I give this land from the River of Egypt [identified by the *Encyclopaedia Judaica* as the Nile River[7]] to the Great River, the river Euphrates, the territory of the Kenites, Kenizzites, Kadmonites, Hittites, Perizzites, Rephaim, Amorites, Canaanites, Girgashites, Hivites, and Jebusites.'

A second territorial description was addressed to those leaving Egypt. It appears in Deuteronomy 1:7-8 and is repeated with slight variations in wording in Deuteronomy 11:24, Joshua 1:4, and Joshua 13:2-5. In this case the extent is from Wadi el Arish (which reaches the Mediterranean Sea in northeastern Sinai) to the northernmost part of the Mediterranean's east coast and eastwards to the Euphrates River. The third category of border description was given to Jews leaving Babylon after the exile there, and it was of a more limited extent: "from Dan to Beersheba" (II Samuel 24:2, I Kings 4:25), and at another time "from the gorge of the Arnon [which empties into the central Dead Sea from the east] as far as Mount Hermon and all the Arabah on the east" (Joshua 12:1). The third category excludes coastal areas settled by Philistines and Phoenicians and includes an area east of the Jordan and the Dead Sea.

According to the *Encyclopaedia Judaica*,[8] the earliest complete description of the territorial extent of the land is found in the book of Numbers, 34:1-12. The description here is very specific and is worth quoting in full.

> The Lord spoke to Moses and said, Give these instructions to the Israelites: Soon you will be entering Canaan. This is the land assigned to you as a perpetual patrimony, the land of Canaan thus defined by its frontiers. Your southern border shall start from the wilderness of Zin, where it marches with Edom, and run southwards from the end of the Dead Sea on its eastern side. It shall then turn from the south up the ascent of Akrabbim and pass by Zin, and its southern limit shall be Kadesh-barnea. It shall proceed by Hazar-addar to Azmon and from Azmon turn towards the Torrent of Egypt, and its limit shall be the sea. Your western frontier shall be the Great Sea and the seaboard; this shall be your frontier to the west. This shall be your northern frontier: you shall draw a line from the Great Sea to Mount Hor and from Mount Hor to Lebo-hamath, and the limit of the frontier shall be Zedad. From there it shall run to Ziphron, and its limit shall be Hazar-enan; this shall be your frontier to the north. To the east you shall draw a line from Hazar-enan to Shepham; it shall run down from Sheham to Riblah east of Ain, continuing until it strikes the ridge east of the sea of Kinnereth. The frontier shall then run down to the Jordan and its limit shall be the Dead Sea. The land defined by these frontiers shall be your land.

This description is considered to be the definition of Canaan, made in a peace treaty between Ramses II and the Hittites about the year 1270 B.C. At the time Canaan was an Egyptian province. It was defined to include all of Palestine except for the southern part, plus today's Lebanon as far as Byblos 20 miles north of Beirut and a large area in southwestern Syria centered on Damascus (Fig. 1). A century later, at the time of the Judges during the 12th century B.C., the area that had come under Israelite control is shown in Figure 2. It

24

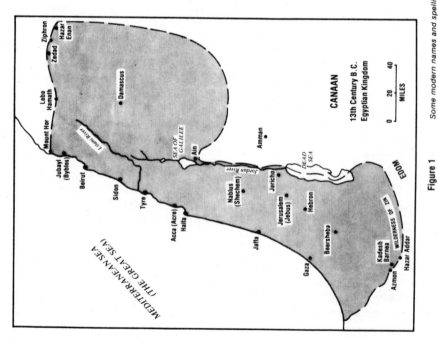

Some modern names and spellings are used for ease of reference.

Figure 1

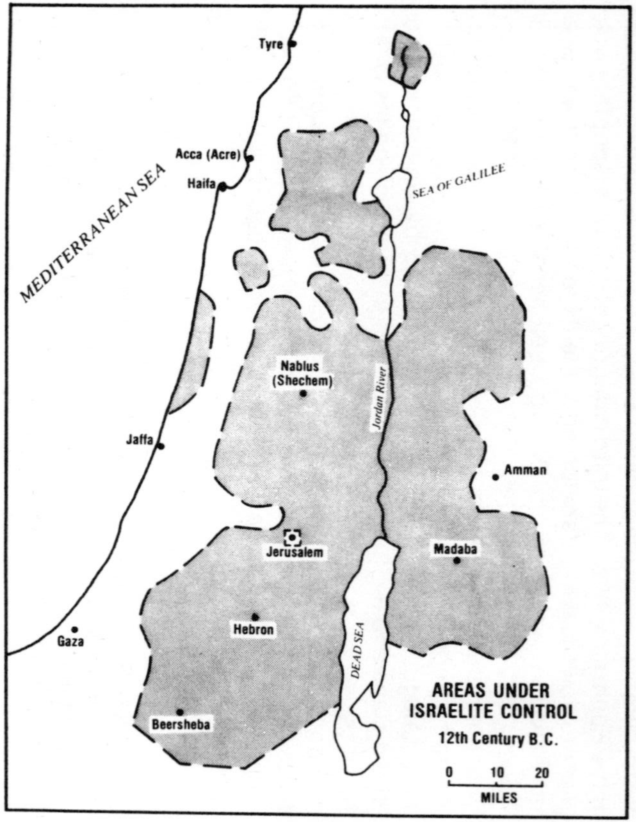

Figure 2

25

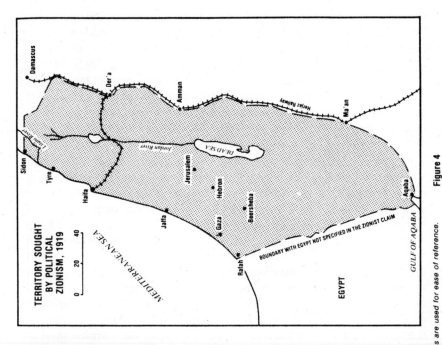

TERRITORY SOUGHT
BY POLITICAL
ZIONISM, 1919

MEDITERRANEAN SEA

Damascus
Der 'a
Amman
Hejaz Railway
Ma an
Sidon
Tyre
Haifa
Jaffa
Gaza
Hebron
Jerusalem
Beersheba
Rafah
DEAD SEA
Jordan River
EGYPT
GULF OF AQABA
Aqaba
BOUNDARY WITH EGYPT NOT SPECIFIED IN THE ZIONIST CLAIM

0 20 40

Figure 4

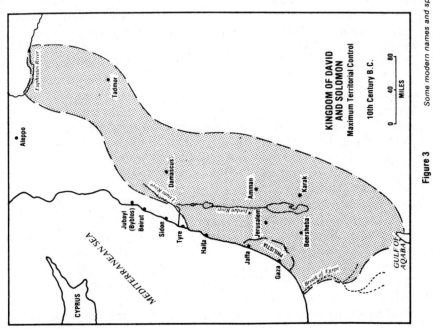

KINGDOM OF DAVID
AND SOLOMON
Maximum Territorial Control
10th Century B.C.

MILES
0 40 80

MEDITERRANEAN SEA

CYPRUS
Aleppo
Tadmor
Euphrates River
Jubayl (Byblos)
Beirut
Sidon
Tyre
Haifa
Jaffa
Damascus
Litani River
Jordan River
Amman
Karak
Jerusalem
Beersheba
Gaza
PHILISTIA
Brook of Egypt
GULF OF AQABA

Figure 3

Some modern names and spellings are used for ease of reference.

25

included much of Palestine, but not the coastal and southern areas, as well as land east of the Jordan to the fringes of the desert. Note the striking correspondence between the control of central Palestine and the area of today's West Bank.[9] In describing this territorial control the *Encyclopaedia Judaica* says: "It is nevertheless evident from the list of unconquered Canaanite cities in Judges 1:21-35 that the ideal and actual limits of Israelite power did not coincide."[10] The encyclopaedia continues to state that "the ideal borders" were almost realized starting with the time of King David (Fig. 3).[11]

Modern political Zionism was organized in 1897 in Basel, Switzerland. It sought to establish a state for Jews in Palestine (though other places were briefly considered). As in the case of Biblical Zionism, the land it sought to acquire was settled by other peoples, and the extent of the land that was sought included both sides of the Jordan valley as well as parts of today's Lebanon and Syria (Fig. 4). Whereas the territorial claim was very specific and detailed in the north and east all the way south to the Gulf of Aqaba, the frontier with Egypt was described as one "to be agreed upon with the Egyptian Government."[12] Ever since the state of Israel was proclaimed on May 14, 1948 it has never had a delimited international boundary. Armistice demarcation lines[13] were established in 1949. These certainly were sharply defined lines, but not boundaries. Lt.-Gen. E.L.M. Burns, who was Chief of Staff of the United Nations Truce Supervision Organization in Palestine from August 1954 to November 1956, observed that "The Arabs are sensitive in regard to the use of the word 'border' or 'boundary' when the demarcation lines are really meant, and always object if these words appear in official documents."[14] The Arab insistence on precise usage was related to the fact that the armistice lines encompassed substantial parts of Palestine that had been conquered by Israel, areas that were additional to those designated by the November 1947 United Nations General Assembly partition resolution as comprising the prospective Jewish state. It should be remembered that the latter designation itself was in dispute because, from the Palestinian perspective, the division was contrary to the will of the country's population in the first place and, moreover, it unfairly allotted a disproportionately large part of Palestine to the minority Jewish population. The term cease fire lines was used following the June 1967 Israeli conquest of the rest of Palestine plus parts of Egypt (Sinai) and Syria (Golan Heights), and following the October 1973 war disengagement lines were marked between Israel and Egypt on the one hand and Israel and Syria on the other. Whereas it is understandable that no international boundaries have ever

marked Israel's territorial extent given the constant state of
belligerency, it is also true that no specific boundary has ever been
designated by any Israeli prime minister, though hints regarding
expectations have been made.

The distinction between what Israel occupies and what Israel
ought to occupy, from the perspective of Israeli and Zionist leaders,
is poignantly revealed in the use of the terms Israel (or State of
Israel) and Eretz Israel (or Land of Israel). The former term refers to
the state as politically constituted and as proclaimed on May 14,
1948. The Hebrew designation of the country is Medinat Israel (the
State of Israel). However, the state, according to the Declaration of
its establishment, was proclaimed to have come into being in only
part of the Land of Israel.[15] For instance, the Declaration states:

> The State of Israel is prepared to cooperate with the agencies and
> representatives of the United Nations in implementing the resolution
> of the General Assembly of the 29th November, 1947, and will take steps
> to bring about the economic union of the whole of Eretz-Israel.[16]

More than a matter of semantics is involved here. When Israeli
officials, and not only Prime Minister Menachem Begin, speak of
Eretz Israel or the Land of Israel they are talking about the
"promised land." Whereas there may be vagueness about the
territorial bounds of the latter,[17] the repeated reference to the Bible
as the deed and as the justification for territorial acquisition is
certainly suggestive. The distinction between the two terms is also
clear, and certainly significant, in a letter written on September 17,
1978 by Prime Minister Menachem Begin to United States President
Jimmy Carter as part of the exchanges that comprised the Camp
David Agreement of September 1978. The letter follows, quoted in full.

Dear Mr. President,

I have the honor to inform you, Mr. President, that on 28 June
1967—Israel's Parliament (The Knesset) promulgated and adopted a
law to the effect: "the Government is empowered by a decree to apply
the law, the jurisdiction and administration of the State to any part of
Eretz Israel (land of Israel—Palestine), as stated in that decree."

On the basis of this law, the Government of Israel decreed in July
1967 that Jerusalem is one city indivisible, the capital of the State of
Israel.

Sincerely,

(signed)

Menachem Begin[18]

The Camp David summit documents also included a September 22, 1978 letter from Carter to Begin which reads as follows, in full.

Dear Mr. Prime Minister:

I hereby acknowledge that you have informed me as follows:

A) In each paragraph of the Agreed Framework Document the expressions "Palestinians" or "Palestinian People" are being and will be construed and understood by you as "Palestinian Arabs."

B) In each paragraph in which the expression "West Bank" appears, it is being, and will be, understood by the Government of Israel as Judea and Samaria.

Sincerely,

(signed)

Jimmy Carter[19]

The phrase Judea and Samaria is part of the Land of Israel as assumed to have been "promised." In May 1979 Israelis celebrated independence day by marching in the West Bank, and Prime Minister Begin repeated his assertion that Jews had the right to settle on Arab lands: "It is completely obvious that we have the right to settle in Eretz Israel."[20]

That Menachem Begin's fanaticism when it comes to land is not merely his but is in fact Israeli policy was illustrated during the March 1979 Knesset debates on the treaty with Egypt that was eventually signed on March 26. For a while there was consternation because of confusion about the wording used in the text of the United States Department of State. The Israeli text said that autonomy would apply to "inhabitants" of the West Bank and Gaza, with no mention of land, and Israelis feared that the Department of State's text might have used "territories" instead of "inhabitants." As it turned out both texts spoke of the objective as being "to provide full autonomy to the inhabitants."[21] The same issue caused delay in the exchange of documents between Egypt and Israel on April 25, 1979 in Sinai.[22] The importance of the matter of wording stems from Israel's interpretation that autonomy would apply to inhabitants while depriving them of their rights to the lands they inhabited and to the waters on these lands. There is a precedent to this distinction between people and their land. When Israel annexed Arab Jerusalem in June 1967, the land was annexed but not the people. For instance, whereas Jerusalem Arabs vote in municipal matters they may not vote in Israeli national elections.[23] Their land, meanwhile, was proclaimed to be Israeli.

In the early 1970s, the head of the Department of Antiquities and Museums of the government of Israel and a former governor of Jerusalem, Avrahan Biran, was asked in an interview, "Do you think archaeology has any relevance to Israel's problems today? Israel is besieged by enemies. What does archaeology have to do with all these? Biran concludes his answer thus:

> It also provides something else. We knew there were Jews in Judea and the Golan Heights, but we did not know, until archaeology produced the evidence, how extensive and for how long the Jewish settlement existed in these parts. The Golan Heights was a thickly inhabited area, and it was inhabited by Jews. We found synagogues, we found schools of learning, we found doorposts, we found gates, we found inscriptions. Settlements today are going up in the Golan Heights. For settlers today it's a continuation of something that was just interrupted. Our God becomes very much alive.[24]

In other words, archaeology serves the state in justifying the retention of conquered territory, a conquest and acquisition justified by reference to God. The phrase "just interrupted" eliminates the relevance of the time factor. Israel has officially wiped out the pre-1967 armistice demarcation lines by prohibiting the sale of maps that show the West Bank as separate from Israel.[25] Meanwhile, Israel has been accelerating the acquisition of Arab lands in the West Bank and Gaza Strip.

It is significant that use of the Old Testament as a basis for trying to ascertain what ought to be the territorial extent of the state of Israel is not limited to Israeli and Zionist theocraticians. At the 1980 annual meeting of the Association of American Geographers one paper addressed the subject "The Land That Yet Remains: Israel's Future Border." It was presented by D. Brooks Green of the Department of Geography at the University of Northern Colorado in Greeley. He examines the boundaries as given in Ezekiel 47:13-21 as "a possible blue-print for predicting the future extent of Israeli control and their expansion into 'the Land that yet remains,' " and he concludes: "We can only watch and see if a war or wars with Lebanon, Syria, and Jordon (sic) permit Israel to extend her northern and eastern borders to those promoted by Ezekiel."[26] Whereas Green makes the disclaimer that his purpose is not to promote the boundary he discusses, the tone of his discussion is anticipatory and sympathetic.

As a political geographer, I must take the Old Testament seriously in order to understand and assess contemporary Israeli policy. The statement "Every place where you set the soles of your feet shall be yours" (Deuteronomy 11:24 and repeated in Joshua 1:3) gives a special significance to the implanting of Jewish settlements on Arab lands: this practice is not subject to negotiation. The Jewish claim is one of divine right; it is a given truth. To the Israeli theocracy Hebron and Nablus are not only as important as Tel Aviv and Haifa, but more important.

2. LAND ACQUISITION

The acquisition of land by the Old Testament Israelites was by conquest. It must be remembered that Jews were not original inhabitants of the land of Canaan. When Abraham migrated from Ur in southern Iraq to Canaan early in the second millennium B.C., already as much known history had taken place in the land of Palestine as has occurred since. In fact God is reported to have told Abraham: "Know this for certain, that your descendants will be aliens living in a land that is not theirs" (Genesis 15:13). The entry of the Jewish migrants from Egypt, under the military leadership of Joshua, was by conquest. Joshua chapter 12 lists thirty-one kings whom the Israelites had to fight during the conquest,[27] first south and east of the Jordan valley and then westwards through Jericho. The conquest was brutal. Moshe Greenburg, Professor of Bible at the Hebrew University of Jerusalem and author of the section on Biblical Judaism in the *Encyclopaedia Britannica*, describes the conquest as "involving both battles of annihilation and treaty arrangements with the natives."[28] Christians are familiar with the story of how Joshua's army blew trumpets and the walls of Jericho collapsed (Joshua 6:20). Hymns of praise and glory celebrate the event. Such jubilation ignores the very next verse: ". . . they destroyed everything in the city; they put everyone to the sword, men and women, young and old, and also cattle, sheep, and asses" (Joshua 6:21). This aspect of the conquest is not often confronted by Christian clergy and lay people. The Old Testament provides numerous examples of Israelite indiscriminate brutality.

> You will soon be crossing the Jordan to enter Canaan. You must drive out all its inhabitants as you advance, destroy all their carved figures and their images of cast metal, and lay their hill-shrines in ruins. You must take possession of the land and settle there, for to you I have given the land to occupy. (Numbers 33:51-53)

When the Lord your God brings you into the land which you are entering to occupy and drives out many nations before you—Hittites, Girgashites, Amorites, Canaanites, Perizzites, Hivites, and Jebusites, seven nations more numerous and powerful than you—when the Lord your God delivers them into your power and you defeat them, you must put them to death. (Deuteronomy 7:1-2)

In the cities of these nations whose land the Lord your God is giving you as patrimony, you shall not leave any creature alive. You shall annihilate them—Hittites, Amorites, Canaanites, Perizzites, Hivites, Jebusites—as the Lord your God commanded you. (Deuteronomy 20:16-17)

So Joshua massacred the population of the whole region—the hill-country, the Negeb, the Shephelah, the watersheds—and all their kings. He left no survivor, destroying everything that drew breath, as the Lord the God of Israel had commanded. Joshua carried the slaughter from Kadesh-barnea to Gaza, over the whole land of Goshen and as far as Gibeon. (Joshua 10:40-41)

It was the Lord's purpose that they should offer an obstinate resistance to the Israelites in battle, and that thus they should be annihilated without mercy and utterly destroyed, as the Lord had commanded Moses. (Joshua 11:20)

The twentieth century Israeli conquest of Palestine also was one of destructive brutality. In 1948-1949 Israel demolished 432 Arab villages. In the subdistrict of Safad, of the 81 existing Arab villages 77 were demolished. In Tiberias subdistrict, 23 out of 25 villages were demolished. In Beisan subdistrict 32 out of 34 were demolished. And so on. This scorched earth practice is even further illustrated by the fact that in that part of Jerusalem subdistrict occupied by Israel in 1948-1949 the density of destruction reached one Arab village per 3.5 square miles.[29] More villages were demolished in 1967, such as the razing of the villages of Yalu, Beit Nuba, and Emwas (Emmaeus).[30] In the seven years following 1967, according to Israeli lawyer Felicia Langer, 19,152 Arab buildings were destroyed, which comes to an average of 53 buildings a week, or more than 7 a day.[31] The breakup and disinheriting of communities in the Negev, which is within the pre-1967 armistice demarcation lines, is one more facet of a deliberate and consistent policy of de-Arabization.[32]

There are other similarities between Biblical and political Zionism in terms of land acquisition. The conquest of Canaan consisted of a series of battles that apparently started at the end of the 14th century B.C. and continued during the 13th century B.C.[33] Contemporary Zionism's acquisition of land started about the beginning of the 20th century, and it is still proceeding with the establishment of Jewish colonial settlements on Arab lands. The destruction of Canaanite towns, according to the *Encyclopaedia Judaica*, did not occur during a short period. The archaeological evidence shows a pattern that "fits into the picture of a gradual Conquest by separate conquering units."[34] Modern Israeli destruction of settlements also is a continuing process. The ancient Israelites failed to conquer the whole country, so that Canaanite enclaves remained and were conquered later.[35] Judges 1:21-35 lists numerous towns that were not subdued, and the phrase "did not drive out" appears half a dozen times, such as in verse 21: "But the Benjamites did not drive out the Jebusites of Jerusalem; and the Jebusites have lived on in Jerusalem till the present day." The lot of many who remained was that the Israelites "put them to forced labour" (e.g. Judges 1:28). Today, the continued presence of a large Arab population in Galilee in pre-1967 Israel, comprising about half the district's population, has been anathema to Israeli officials. Israel Koenig, Commissioner of the Northern District for Israel's Ministry of Interior, submitted in 1976 to the Prime Minister a plan that would decrease the Arab presence and increase the Jewish presence in the region.[36] The March 10, 1978 *Jerusalem Post* reported that the military government had decided to change the status of the Gaza Strip to a district instead of an administered territory.[37] The October 20, 1981 *Des Moines* (Iowa) *Register* reported the appointment by Israel of the first civilian administrator of the occupied West Bank, effective October 30, 1981. On December 14, 1981 the Israeli parliament approved a bill that proclaimed the annexation of Syria's Golan Heights, and it is significant to note the "Eretz Israel" justification by Prime Minister Menachem Begin. According to United Press International:

> Begin said the Golan Heights, occupied by Israel in 1967, has always been part of the historic Land of Israel and only "colonial arbitrariness" has caused its separation from the rest of Palestine after World War I.
> "This arbitrariness is not binding on us. Historically, the Golan Heights was and will be an integral part of Eretz Israel (the Land of Israel)," Begin said.[38]

The ancient Israelites were aided by "Egypt's inability to deal with specific problems of Canaan," so that the population of Canaan was "defenseless" against the invaders.[39] Palestinian Arabs were defenseless against the Zionist forces before Israel declared itself a

state on May 14, 1948, so that by April 1948 there had already been
300,000 displaced Arabs, and after Israel's statehood the defense-
lessness became even more pathetic. The role of Egypt also has
curious geopolitical trans-temporal parallels. A February 1949 issue
of the *Jerusalem Post*, after Egypt became the first Arab country to
conclude an armistice agreement following the 1948-1949 war,
stated: "Egypt has separated itself from the other Arab states and
recognized the state of Israel."[40] This statement could apply
verbatim to the Egypt-Israel agreement of March 1979 following the
September 1978 Camp David Summit. Egypt remains unable to deal
with the specific problems of Palestinians. The subjugation of the
Canaanites did not mean that peace followed. On the contrary, the
Israelites were in frequent conflict with adjacent peoples, such as
the Midianites (Judges 6:3-5; 7-12) and the Ammonites (Judges
10:17ff). Similarly, today's Israel has been in frequent conflict with
neighbors. Necessarily, and irrespective of the extent of military
success, there will always be a periphery on the other side of which
there will be peoples who will continue to retaliate. According to the
Jewish Encyclopedia: "Against the more numerous and wealthy but
divided Canaanites the main advantage possessed by the Hebrews
was common action over an extended area inspired by land-hunger
and by religious enthusiasm."[41] Today we see division among Arab
states, some of which are wealthy, and we see a land-hungry Israel
hastily spreading colonial settlements on Arab lands and working
hard to Judaize Arab areas, both within pre-1967 Israel, such as
Galilee,[42] and in the occupied West Bank and Gaza Strip.

3. EXCLUSIVISM

The ancient Israelites had clear instructions from God that they
were to keep themselves separate from other peoples. "You must
not intermarry with them, neither giving your daughters to their
sons nor taking their daughters for your son" (Deuteronomy 1:3).
"Be on your guard then, love the Lord your God, for if you do turn
away and attach yourselves to the peoples that will remain among
you, and intermarry with them and they with you, then be sure that
the Lord will not continue to drive those peoples out to make room
for you" (Joshua 23:11-13). "Foreigners shall rebuild your walls and
their kings shall be your servants" (Isaiah 60:10). The exclusivism is
part of the covenant with God, with whom Jews had a special
relationship as the "chosen people." The covenant would be
affirmed by the carrying out of a specific physical ritual.

God said to Abraham, 'For your part, you must keep my covenant, and you and your descendants after you, generation by generation. This is how you shall keep my covenant between myself and you and your descendants after you: circumcise yourselves, every male among you. You shall circumcise the flesh of your foreskin, and it shall be the sign of the covenant between us. Every male among you in every generation shall be circumcised on the eighth day, both those born in your house and any foreigner, not of your blood but bought with your money. Circumcise both those born in your house and those bought with your money. Every uncircumcised male, everyone who has not had the flesh of his foreskin circumcised, shall be cut off from the kin of his father. He has broken my covenant.' (Genesis 17:9-14)

The insistence on this particular physical sign of Jewishness may appear curious because of the fact that Jewishness of the newborn is determined by motherhood and not by fatherhood: a Jew is one born to a Jewish mother, irrespective of who the father is, but not vice versa. (One can also become a Jew if converted.) According to the Talmud: "thy son by an Israelite woman is called thy son, but thy son by a heathen is not called thy son."[43] This requirement of maternal rather than paternal lineage makes it possible to ascertain parentage: whereas there may be question about who the father is, this is not so with the mother. Thus the "chosenness" is safeguarded and exclusivism is maintained.

Today, the essential Jewishness of the state of Israel is instutitutionally promulgated. It is exemplified by the Law of Return, which proclaims:

1. Every Jew has the right to immigrate to this country.

. . . .

4. Every Jew who immigrated to this country before the commencement of this Law and every Jew born in the country, whether before or after the commencement of this Law, is in the same position as one who immigrated under this Law.

4A. (a) The rights of a Jew . . . are also granted to the child and grandchild of a Jew, to the spouse of a Jew and to the spouse of the child and grandchild of a Jew—with the exception of a person who was a Jew and willingly changed his religion. . . .

4B. For the purpose of this Law, "a Jew" means a person born to a Jewish mother or converted to Judaism and who is not a member of another religion.[44]

At first reading this law seems reasonable enough, for after all Israel is a Jewish state, and one of its primary functions is to provide refuge for world Jewry. What is disturbing, however, is that it is a Jewishness established in a land of non-Jews, and it is a Jewishness institutionalized for Jews, so that within the state system non-Jews are the outsiders; they simply do not belong in the system. There is an abundant literature about the legally institutionalized discrimination against non-Jews, and of course here the referent is the Arab population. One study will be noted here, a serious volume entitled *The Population of Israel* and coauthored by two demographers at the Hebrew University in Jerusalem.[45] Chapter 5 deals with natality. An active pronatalist policy for Israeli Jews, but not for Israeli Arabs, has been of such great concern to Israel that a Natality Committee was eventually appointed in 1962, responsible directly to the Prime Minister. "The offices [of the special body that would deal with the general questions of natality] were to be located within the Prime Minister's office, although at least one member of the Natality Committee suggested that the Jewish Agency might be a more appropriate location, since the policy was intended to increase Jewish fertility and not the fertility of the total population."[46] The phrase "population problem," used several times in the book, has a special meaning to Israel: the presence of non-Jews.

Israel's zealousness about its Jewishness and concern lest its Jews may change their religion led to the passage on December 27, 1977 of a law against missionary activity, to take effect April 1, 1978.

> He who gives or promises to give money, an equivalent of money, or other benefit in order to entice a person to change his religion, or in order to entice a person to bring about the change of another's religion, his sentence will be five years imprisonment, or a fine of IL50,000.
>
> He who receives or agrees to receive money, an equivalent of money, or a benefit in exchange for a promise to change his religion, or to bring about the change of another's religion, the sentence due to him is three years imprisonment, or a fine of IL30,000.[47]

In other words, it is a criminal offense to propagate one's faith or to change one's religion.

Another comparison between Biblical and political Zionism, in terms of the fundamental exclusivism of both, involves the question of land. "No land shall be sold outright, because the land is mine" (Leviticus 25:23). Today land is held by the State or by the Jewish Agency in perpetuity for the Jewish people. For instance, a kibbutz does not own the land it cultivates. It owns the cucumbers and the tomatoes, but the land is leased from the state. If land is designated as Jewish, one may ask, why not permit, in fact encourage, Jewish ownership of land? The reason is to forestall the possibility of a future sale, whether by the owner or by a descendant, to a non-Jew. In the West Bank and Gaza, territories under Israeli military occupation, Israel insists on the right of Jews to colonize Arab lands but does not permit the repatriation of Arabs to these same lands. This is not surprising, for how else could the land be so easily expropriated for Jews and alienated from Arabs?

Israel and its driving force Zionism are not anti-Arab, or anti-Palestinian. They are anti-non-Jewish. It was the lot of Palestinian Arabs to be the inhabitants of the targeted territory.

4. DIVINE RIGHT AND HOLY WAR

In high school history we study about the concept of a divine right of kings, whereby the king is the final authority on the divine nature of his power. Fortunately, the concept of a divine right of kings has gone out of the historical window. Unfortunately, the claim of a divine right to someone else's land still endures. Menachem Begin, the Israeli government, and the Zionist political movement have taken the position: your land is my land because I am a Jew and you are not. God says so, and I know what God thinks. Perceiving God as a real estate agent reduces to absurdity the concept of a just and loving God. Equally absurd is the waging of war with the presumption of God's "blessing," and sometimes by opposing armies in the same battle.

This leads to reflections on the matter of holy wars. Holy wars have not been limited to any one people, or to any one religion, or to any one period. In terms of the comparison here made between Biblical and political Zionism, both Zionisms waged holy wars: they proclaimed a divine justification and authority for claiming someone else's territory, and both waged wars to achieve the objectives. In the case of Biblical Zionism there is a unique aspect to its holy war. The divine right to the land of Canaan was atemporal. It was retrospective, starting at the beginning of time, even though the Jews were not in that land. Furthermore, the divine right to land applied forever more, irrespective of whether or not Jews were in the land. It was eternal, in both historical directions. Hence, the holy war waged by twentieth century political Zionism makes sense in this perceived divine order of things. It could have been waged anytime, irrespective of conditions in Palestine, whether political or demographic, because the divine justification would always be invoked as eternally valid. The brutality of Jewish vigilantes in the West Bank, such as members of the Gush Emunim, and in the Negev, such as the Green Squad, is seen as sanctioned by divine will. One member of Gush Emunim told a journalist:

> [W]e are dedicated to one goal: to drive the Arabs out of Greater Israel. . . . We do not see lines on a map. The border will be made after we settle the area. In every place where we make a settlement we will never abandon that settlement. We know all of Israel's towns and villages have been founded on what once were Arab towns and villages. We want all the Arabs to leave, and if coming to settle here means we must be in a continual state of warfare with the Arabs, then so be it. If we can't have a Greater Israel, then we don't want peace.[48]

Another Gush Emunim settler in the Arab West Bank says: "We believe it is important for Jews to live in our own land, in Judea and Samaria [West Bank]. We were promised all this by God." And this promise, he added, included the country of Jordan east of the Jordan River.[49]

A similarly outspoken position has been actively pursued by Rabbi Meir Kahane. Kahane, an American, was founder of the Jewish Defense League. He went to Israel where his zealot anti-Arabism became a public nuisance that led to his imprisonment. He wrote a book, entitled *They Must Go*,[50] in which he described Israel's Arab population as a cancer within Israel, one that must be removed. Eliminating the Arab presence, by forcible expulsion if need be, is not merely a political issue: it is a religious obligation for the sake of Israel's redemption and for the sanctity of the name of the God of Israel.

DIVINE COVENANT OR FOLK LITERATURE?

In my reading of the Old Testament I find a contradiction between the covenant with Abraham and the covenant with Moses. In Genesis 17:8 God tells Abraham: "As an everlasting possession I will give you and your descendants after you the land in which you are now aliens, all the land of Canaan, and I will be God to your descendants." (Genesis 23 narrates how Abraham requested from his Canaanite hosts the acquisition of a piece of land to bury his wife Sarah.) The covenant with Moses included the Ten Commandments, the tenth of which enjoined: "Thou shalt not covet thy neighbor's house . . . nor any thing that is thy neighbor's" (Exodus 20:17, King James version). But Abraham was at liberty to covet things that were his neighbor's, and in fact he was authorized by God to do so. Today's Israel also regards the Abrahamic covenant as a license to covet, to take over, and to retain.

At the outset I said I was a political geographer and not a theologian. I have no difficulty viewing the Old Testament as the folk literature of a people. At the same time I know that some view it as sacred prophetic literature, and act accordingly. In terms of the history of the land of Palestine such belief has led to frequent strife, to holy wars. This was true of Biblical Zionism. It is true of contemporary political Zionism.[51] The tragedy of Zionism, both Biblical and modern, is the perception of God as an earthly political leader, interested in power and land as much as in the spiritual welfare of men and women.

NOTES

1. *The Jewish Encyclopedia*. Funk and Wagnalls Company, New York, 1925, Vol. XII, p. 666.
2. *Encyclopaedia Judaica*, Keter Publishing House, Ltd., 1971, Vol. 16, Col. 1032. (This encyclopaedia is numbered by columns rather than by pages.)
3. *The Jewish Encyclopedia*, Vol. IV, p. 319.
4. *Encyclopaedia Judaica*, Vol. 5, Col. 1018.
5. Biblical quotations are taken from *The New English Bible*, New York: Oxford University Press, and Cambridge University Press, 1970.
6. *Encyclopaedia Judaica*, Vol. 9, Col. 112.
7. Ibid.
8. Ibid., Col. 114.
9. An intriguing comparison between the core of Israelite territorial control during Old Testament times and the 1949 cease fire line between Israel and Jordan is made in Denis Baly, *Geographical Companion to the Bible*, New York: McGraw-Hill, 1963, pp. 58–59.
10. *Encyclopaedia Judaica*, Vol. 9, Cols. 114–115.
11. Ibid., Col. 115.
12. The full text of the territorial claim is given in Meyer W. Weisgal, general editor. *The Letters and Papers of Chaim Weizmann*, Jerusalem: Israel Universities Press, 1977, Vol. IX, Series A, p. 392.
13. United Nations. *Treaty Series*. Volume 42, 1949. Treaty No. 656, p. 312.
14. E. L. M. Burns. *Between Arab and Israeli*. New York: Iran Obolensky, Inc., 1963, p. 297, note. 10.
15. "Declaration of the Establishment of Israel, May 14, 1948." In John Norton Moore, editor, *The Arab-Israeli Conflict: Readings and Documents*, Princeton, New Jersey: Princeton University Press, 1977, pp. 934–937.

16. Ibid., p. 936.

17. A discussion of territorial claims made by various leading Zionists (for instance including David Ben Gurion) is found in Israel Shahak. "The Historical Right and the Other Holocaust," *Journal of Palestine Studies*, Vol. X, No. 3, Spring 1981, pp. 27–34, esp. 28–32.

18. Department of State, *The Camp David Summit: September 1978*, Publication 8954, Near East and South Asian Series 88, September 1978, p. 14.

19. Ibid., p. 15.

20. Associated Press, *Des Moines Register*, May 3, 1979, p. 2.

21. "Joint Letter to President Carter from President Sadat and Prime Minister Begin," *The Egyptian-Israeli Peace Treaty, March 26, 1979*, Washington, D.C., The Department of State, Selected Documents No. 11, April 1979.

22. "An Unpromising Start for Peace," *Time*, Vol. 113, No. 19, May 7, 1979, p. 35.

23. Don Peretz, "The War Election and Israel's Eighth Knesset," *Middle East Journal*, Vol. 28, No. 2, Spring 1974, p. 124.

24. "Why Excavate in Israel?" *Johns Hopkins Magazine*, Vol XXIV, No. 1, March 1973, p. 2.

25. Elizabeth Monroe, "The West Bank: Palestinian or Israeli?" *Middle East Journal*, Vol. 31, No. 4, Autumn 1977, p. 406.

26. D. Brooks Green, "The Land That Yet Remains: Israel's Future Border." March 26, 1979. Manuscript, pp. ii and 13.

27. The count is given in *Encyclopaedia Judaica*, Vol. 5. Col. 100.

28. *Encyclopedia Britannica*, Macropaedia, Vol. 10, p. 305.

29. These figures are from a forthcoming book by Bishara Muammar and Basheer K. Nijim about population changes in Palestine/Israel. The study was funded by the American Palestine Education Foundation, Washington, D.C.

30. Amos Kenan, "Report on the Razing of Villages and the Expulsion of Refugees," in *Arab Areas Occupied by Israel in June, 1967*. Association of Arab-American University Graduates, Information Papers No. 2, September 1970, pp. 36–37.

31. Felicia Langer, "Israeli Violation of Human Rights in the Occupied Arab Territories," in *Palaces of Injustice*, New York: Americans for Middle East Understanding, 1976, p. 24.

32. See for instance Kurt Goering, "Israel and the Bedouin of the Negev," *Journal of Palestine Studies*, Vol. IX, No. 1, Autumn 1979, pp. 3–20.

33. *Encyclopaedia Judaica*, Vol. 8, Col. 577.

34. Ibid., Cols. 578-579.

35. Ibid., Col. 579.

36. "A Secret Document," in *Palaces of Injustice*, New York: Americans for Middle East Understanding, 1976. This publication contains the full text of the *Memorandum Proposal—Handling the Arabs of Israel—General*, pp. 6–21. The text was published in the Israeli daily newspaper *Al-Hamishmar*, September 7, 1976 and was translated to English by Israel Shahak who added explanatory footnotes.

37. *Al-Ittihad* (Arabic language newspaper), Haifa, March 14, 1978.

38. "Israel votes to annex Golan Heights; Syria cancels ceasefire," *The* (Cedar Falls, Iowa) *Record*, December 15, 1981, p. 1.

39. *Encyclopaedia Judaica*, Vol. 8, Col. 580.

40. Quoted in David Hirst, "Sadat Versus the Arabs," *Middle East International*, No. 96, 30 March 1979, p. 5.

41. *The Jewish Encyclopedia*, Vol. VI, p. 663.

42. Israel Shahak, ed., *The Non-Jew in the Jewish State*, Jerusalem, 1975, Chapter III: "The Official Policy of Judaization: Examples," pp. 61–78. See also "A Secret Document," note 36 above.

43. Kiddushin 68b. Source used: *The Babylonian Talmud*, I. Epstein translator, London: The Soncino Press, 1936, p. 345.

44. "The Law of Return, 1950, as Amended in 1954 and 1970," in John Norton Moore, op. cit. (note 15), p. 991.

45. Dov Friedlander and Calvin Goldscheider, *The Population of Israel*, New York: Columbia University Press, 1979. Friedlander is associate professor in the departments of demography and statistics and director of the Levi Eshkol Institute for Economic, Social, and Political Research at the Hebrew University, Jerusalem. Goldscheider is chairman and associate professor in the department of demography at the Hebrew University.

46. Ibid., p. 133.

47. "Penal Code Amendment Law (Enticement to Change of Religion) 1977." *Knesset Gazette* (Draft Laws) No. 1313. Reproduced in *The Link*, Vol. 11, No. 2, Mid-Spring, 1978, p. 2.

48. Grace Halsell, *Journey to Jerusalem*, New York: Macmillan Publishing Co., 1981, p. 47.

49. Ibid., p. 52.

50. Rabbi Meir Kahane, *They Must Go*, New York: Grosset & Dunlap, 1981.

51. In 1969 I argued that even if the state of Israel were to cease to exist, whether by peaceful or violent means, "the 'Palestine problem' will still not be resolved, because Zionism itself will not cease with the non-existence of a state of Israel. Consequently, once more there will be a yearning for the resurrection of a secular state in the 'Promised Land.' Yet, and once more again, there will be opposition by the indigenous population to what to them will be an alien intrusion." Basheer K. Nijim, "Israel and the Potential for Conflict," *The Professional Geographer*, Vol. XXI, No. 5, September 1969, p. 323.

MAP SOURCES

The maps in figures 1-4 are based on information from the following sources.

Denis Baly, *The Geography of the Bible*, New York: Harper & Row, 1974.

Denis Baly and A. D. Tushingham, *Atlas of the Biblical World*, New York: World Publishing Company, 1971.

Encyclopaedia Judaica, Keter Publishing House, Ltd., 1971, Vol. 9, columns 112-115, 316.

Survey of Israel, *Atlas of Israel*, Amsterdam: Elsevier Publishing Company, 1970, Map IX/4.

3

Zionism: Redemption or Retrogression?

Rabbi Elmer Berger

I

RELIGION VS. NATIONALISM

Two popular misconceptions, both cultivated by Zionist propaganda, have inhibited experts in the humanity-sciences from applying to critiques of Zionism and its Middle Eastern state the generally accepted criteria of their disciplines. The first misconception is that this political/national movement and ideology which spawned the State of Israel is identical with, or at least integral to, the historic religion of Judaism. The second inhibiting misrepresentation is that Zionism is a "liberation" movement, a force for releasing and emancipating human spirit, or at least the spirit of Jews.

There is no lack of Jews, Christians, Moslems and non-believers who dispute these Zionist assertions. In recent months an increasing number have "gone public," systematically verbalizing their disagreement. But the impact of their efforts on American and West European decision-makers has, so far, been minimal.

One explanation I believe is that, responsible and accurate as they may be with facts, critics very often submit their evidence in ways which are too episodic and disjointed. There is an abundance of damaging evidence but the scatter-gun presentations make it easy for Zionist apologists to explain that the incidents are "selective" and represent either eccentricities or temporary measures adopted with reluctance in the interests of "defending" the Zionist state against implacably hostile neighbors. There is a current trend to assign most of Israel's objectionable policies to Menachem Begin, as if he is some surprising, unpredictable "extreme," instead of the authentic disciple of Herzlian Zionism he is.

A more specific example of a well-documented indictment of Israeli policy turned aside and covered over with the apologia that the situation was not typical was the report of Ms. Alexandra U. Johnson, an American diplomat, exposing examples of torture practiced by the Israeli authorities on Palestinians in the occupied territories.[1] The report was almost cavalierly dismissed with only perfunctory attention by both official Washington and the American media.

The official response of the Department of State admitted there was truth to the Johnson charges. But it skirted the issue by arguing there was not sufficient evidence to indict the Israeli government for pursuing the practices as a "systematic" policy.

The fact is that the conditions Ms. Johnson reported and most of the other actions of the Zionist Movement and Israel which are frequent subjects of condemnation—often at the level of United Nations resolutions—are merely visible symptoms of fundamental Zionist values and ideology. These values and this ideology are incompatible with Judaism or with the value-system of valid perceptions of most contemporary religions. Zionism's "eccentricities" or "unavoidable defense" measures must be understood as cultivated actions, pre-determined by the historic development of authentic Zionist policy and ideology. Only with such in-depth comprehension will they command sufficient, sustained attention to cope with them in ways designed either to eliminate them or at least to neutralize them so they no longer present obstacles to peace.

Some simplified, philosophical definitions will facilitate making the distinction between Zionism and Judaism. The first is that the ultimate objective of *any* religion worthy of the name must be the greatest possible release and freedom of the human spirit. But any authentic religion, whether through the preachings of Jesus or emulation of Muhammad or in Judaism the demands of the Covenant, enjoins that this freedom of the spirit is realized only by acceptance of disciplines.

Too often institutionalized forms of the great religions have become earthbound because the disciplines are confused with the goals. But this does not invalidate the religion. It merely indicts the pygmy vision of those who pronounce sacred what should never have been regarded as more than the servants of sanctity. This elusive character of the ultimate of authentic religions explains the great prophets in all of them who spoke in absolutes; and why the sum total of their absolutes was called God. It also explains why searchers for God in all of the great faiths were hesitant to list the attributes of God.

None of these authentic religious attributes applies to the state. Religion's ultimate purpose is to serve God by inspiring man to continuous struggle for the unattainable. The state's function is to serve *man* and, in less commendable forms of statehood, to have man serve the state. Politicians may employ pietistic exhortations to justify political action. But the tools of politicians are compromises with man's limitations and sometimes even with his evil. The success of the state is measured by the comfort and pacification of its inhabitants. The success of authentic religion is measured by the agony of the spirit which knows it has not achieved perfection and is uncomfortable in the presence of compromise even with the good.

Drawing these boundaries with even a broad brush is essential to analyzing Zionism's strategy for exploiting Judaism to serve the ends of Zionist statehood.

II

ZIONIST SPECIFICS

It is logical to begin with Theodor Herzl. And from Herzl's writings it is also logical to select *The Jewish State*, the classic of political/territorial Zionism. The central thesis of the founder of modern Zionism is that anti-Semitism is endemic and ineradicable. In the Preface to the book, Herzl says the central idea is

[A]n ancient one: It is the restoration of the Jewish State.[2]

Herzl was convinced that the dynamic which would translate his central idea into reality was that

The world resounds with clamor against the Jews, and this has revived the dominant idea.

Herzl had an answer for those who might consider his idea Utopian.

Am I ahead of my time? Are the sufferings of Jews not yet acute
enough? We shall see.[3]

And further:

. . . [T]he longer anti-Semitism lies dormant, the more violently will it
erupt.[4]

And finally,

I shall now put the question in the briefest possible form: Shouldn't we
"get out" at once, and if so, whither? Or, may we remain, and if so, how
long?[5]

This fundamental conceptualization of Zionism is wholly at
variance with authentic religious aspiration. In theological terms
Herzl was saying that evil—the evil of anti-Semitism—is immutable.
His political projection allows for no hope of human spiritual
development and redemption.

III

ZIONIST DECEPTIONS

Later Zionist strategists—and apologists—attempted to diminish
the importance Herzl attached to anti-Semitism as the dynamic of
the movement. But simply as an affirmative, motivating aspiration,
Zionism's territorial nationalism had no appreciable number of
proponents among Jews. Having launched the movement with the
éclat of the First Zionist Congress it became an integral part of
Zionist strategy to denigrate and demean emancipation and even to
obstruct it where possible.

Chaim Weizmann knew Jews better than Herzl. He knew even the
less fortunate Jews of Central and Eastern Europe. By 1907
Weizmann was complaining to the 9th Congress:

The Jewish people has not yet shown that it has a will.[6]

The Balfour Declaration and the diplomacies at the end of World
War I which incorporated the Declaration in the Palestine Mandate
did little to bolster Zionist confidence in the authenticity of their

claims to represent "the Jewish people." On March 5, 1919, Weizmann reported to the International Zionist Conference in London the experiences of the Zionist delegation to Paris. One part of his report is revealing. "The French Government" had informed the Zionist delegation that, in addition to the Zionist spokesmen, Mr. Sylvain Levi had been invited to represent "the French Jews." Weizmann observed:

> This rather disconcerted us and we rang up the French Government . . . inquiring whom Mr. Levi represented. The reply was given that Mr. Levi represented the French Jews.

The next morning the Zionists contacted Mr. Levi and informed him

> [W]e felt very embarrassed, not because we thought he had made any great impression on the Conference, but we felt his interposition to have been a *Hillul Hashem*.[7] (A blasphemy.)

Later, with the Mandate in effect and what Weizmann called "practical work" under way, the wily President of the Zionist Organization—speaking to a banquet of Zionists in far off Rumania—could confess what a fraud had been perpetrated a decade earlier.

> [W]e are the greatest war profiteers,

he said. And added,

> The Balfour Declaration of 1917 was built on air, and a foundation had to be laid for it through years of exacting work; every day and every hour of these last ten years, when opening the newspapers, I thought: Whence will the next blow come? I trembled lest the British Government would call me and ask: "Tell us, what is this Zionist Organization? Where are they, your Zionists?"—The Jews, they knew, were against us; we stood alone on a little island, a tiny group of Jews with a foreign past.[8]

This belated confession of arrogation reveals a classical Zionist strategy. What Mr. Dayan repeatedly describes as "establishing facts" is only a new label for Zionism's historic politics of deceit, of deliberate ambiguity and consciously inflated claims. By whatever name, it cannot be reconciled with religion, even though more often than it should it is countenanced in statecraft.

And one final, *post facto* confession of political chicanery which, for their own imperial reasons, was gullibly or cynically accepted by the so-called "Great Powers." Addressing the 17th Zionist Congress, in Basel in 1931, Weizmann recalled the days when he and his colleagues were negotiating the Balfour Declaration. He confessed:

> In these initial days, when the relationship was slowly taking shape and finding expression in international agreements, I often asked myself what we—I and my friends who were speaking for the Jewish people—could answer were we asked to "show our credentials"—to prove our right to act as the representative of world Jewry. That no such question was ever put is perhaps the strongest proof of the intuitive understanding of those men who spoke with us on behalf of Great Britain, and who saw us, not as the nominated or elected representatives of this or that group, but as the spokesmen of a people in the making. And this attitude is the more surprising when one remembers that the so-called "big Jews," and the official Jews, were then very strongly opposed to Zionist ideals and aspirations.[9]

IV

MAKING "GOOD" ON THE LIES

But the Zionist managers knew that, eventually, "the truth will out." Techniques, artifices, devices had to be invented to conceal the insubstantiality of their phantom constituency. One technique designed to mollify anti-Zionist Jews was to suppress the use of the word "state." In his report to the same London conference in 1919 in which Weizmann had complained about Sylvain Levi, he also reported that the French government had issued "an official statement to the Press" which "said that France would not oppose the placing of Palestine under British trusteeship and the formation of a Jewish State." Weizmann added,

> The use of the words "Jewish State" was significant, as we had refrained from using them.[10]

By avoiding public disclosure of its ultimate objective, Zionism could portray itself as an amorphous mixture of humanitarianism, culture, economic development. It could be marketed as having something for everyone and it could be all things to all people. It could fool some of "the Arabs" and it could certainly fool most of the

Jews who were thousands of miles away. George Antonius reports how the first King Husain—speaking for Arabs who were still naive about Zionism—was tricked by the Zionists and the British when news of the Balfour Declaration leaked. Commander Hogarth went to Jedda in January, 1918, and assured Husain,

> Jewish *settlement* in Palestine would only be allowed insofar as would be consistent with *the political and economic freedom of the Arab population.*[11]   (Emphasis by Antonius.)

To which Husain, according to Antonius, offered the "explicit" reply:

> [T]hat in so far as the aim of the Balfour Declaration was to provide a refuge to Jews from persecution, he would use all his influence to further that aim.[12]

Antonius further reports that Husain "ordered his sons to do what they could to allay the apprehensions caused by the Balfour Declaration among their followers." Menachem Begin's philandering with the term "autonomy" therefore has solid, Zionist precedent reaching back to the wiliest Zionist of them all. And Jimmy Carter's condescension to the Palestinians, offering them a muffled voice in determining their own destiny, has an unflattering precedent in British duplicity more than half a century ago.

It was even easier to fool non-Palestinian Jews with such semantic trickery. Samuel Halperin's definitive book, appropriately titled *The Political World of American Zionism*,[13] is about as exhaustive an examination as there is of the devices and propaganda employed by the Zionist apparatus to snare American Jews into that "political world" without revealing they were becoming netted in big and complicated politics. Adolph Hitler's contribution to the creation of the Zionist state is widely recognized. Less familiar, as Halperin puts it, is that "many a Zionist leader" found "Jewish support" for Zionism motivated by "philanthropy and compassion" to be something other than an "unmixed blessing."[14] Zionist misgivings about the conversion of American Jews to a Zionism masked with what authentic Zionists called "refugeeism" involved more than mere ideological puritanism. The danger was that the world might find humanitarian answers for the Jewish victims of the Nazis. In 1936, virtually an entire program at a National Conference for Palestine in New York was devoted to making the clarification. Throughout February of 1936, the official organ of the Zionist Organization of America, *New Palestine*, prominently featured statements by Abba Hillel Silver, Weizmann, and Stephen Wise. Silver exhorted the Conference

> Let us not lose sight in this hour of tribulation of the basic and the classic ideals of our movement.
>
> Zionism was more than an escape from persecution. . . . It was a movement toward national auto-emancipation.[15]

These were disclosures to a fraternal audience. But even there—to an audience of *American Zionists*—it is at least doubtful many of them really comprehended the meaning of such language as "national auto-emancipation."

V

ENOUGH DERELICTIONS FOR ALL

This speaking with forked tongues, this duplicity, this concealment of motivation and ultimate objectives was not unique to Zionism as a *political* movement. The same was—and is—done every day by governments and the world's leading political figures and by its political pygmies, as well. And if the run-of-the-mine electorates living under governments led by these paragons of leadership are unsure of what these governments and leaders mean it was no different with the garden-variety Jews of the United States. They simply did not—and do not even now—understand the artfully designed Zionist lingo.

I can find excuses in my heart and mind for the Jewish shoe salesman, or taxi driver, or department store magnate who simply went along with Zionism out of a sense of responsibility for the endangered lives of other Jews. But I find no mercy for the rabbis, the social scientists, the well-paid executives of Jewish organizations who spent every hour of their working days specializing in "Jewish" problems and who were taken for the ride. And I find even less excuse for those in these specializing groups who knew better, who were opposed to the whole process of Zionizing the status and destiny of Jews but who were dissuaded from sharing their knowledge by pressures, name-calling, power-seeking and other persuaders common to the *political* millieu. I also find little reason to excuse the Christian counterparts of these specialists in so-called "Jewish" affairs. Too many of them were—and still are—

excessively guilty accomplices *after* the fact. This synthetic, superficially constructed facade of Christian approval legitimated Zionism or at least pro-Zionism for many Jews. If the predominant Christian leadership in America had investigated Zionism, listened to their own experts who had served as missionaries and educators in the Middle East, they could not—as genuine Christians—have made it so easy for Zionism to have so easily had its way with American Jews. For as there were Jews, so there were Christians who knew with certainty that Zionism, to realize its muted but never surrendered ultimate objectives, required a usurpation of Palestinian rights and the dehumanizing of Palestine's indigenous people.

And finally, in almost any religious scale of moral responsibility, the lowest level of respect and honor is assigned to the political leaders of this nation. They all had experts thirty years ago—and if such evidence as the King-Crane Commission is admissible, then half a century ago—who advised that American support of Zionism was contrary to this nation's interests and inconsistent with American democratic values.

There is nothing in this scenario which suggests that practitioners of high religion, reciting the beatitudes of Christianity or the more passionate and perhaps more sociologically-oriented moral absolutes of the Old Testament prophets, played or made serious effort to play an effective and decisive role. It is almost blasphemous that it has taken half a century and a dependency upon Arab oil even now to send some of these believers back to their spiritual drawing-boards to study what Zionism intended all along.

VI

ZIONIST ENERGY—ARAB DERELICTIONS

It is important that we who are still grappling with this problem realize the Zionist machine was no *passive* recipient of the political advantages which accrued to this combination of ignorance, crowd-pleasing and moral turpitude. Whatever Zionism reaped was, in no small part, the result of what it had sown. At every stage of Zionist expansionism they pursued their *fait accompli* diplomacy and economics. From the provocative Rutenberg Concessions of the 1920s to the insidious violations of the country's recognized institutions in the so-called "Wailing Wall" incidents, to the illegal immigrations, to the unilateral declaration of the establishment of the Zionist state despite second thoughts at the United Nations in

1947-48, to the deliberate terrorizing of the Palestinian Arabs by Mr.
Begin's Irgunists, creating the first "refugee" problem, to the "pre-
emptive" war of 1967 and the weaseling about the meaning of the
language of Resolution 242 and the subsequent, current diplomacy
of holding hostage land which it is "inadmissible" for them to hold
because it was acquired by war, the Zionist movement and its state
have relentlessly and single-mindedly pursued the unspoken or, at
best, stage-whispered goal. Through it all there was on the part of
the Zionist movement what someone has called "the-will-to-
deceive." The patron-powers exhibited a corresponding willingness to be deceived. Among American Jews generally, as throughout much of the rest of the world, there was indifference, ignorance
and, among some, the attitude of moderately interested spectators.
These were willing to pay the professionals running the Zionist
apparatus as a kind of price for a ticket to a spectator sport.

None of this is meant as an apologia for either Jewish or Christian
religionists who either actively supported Zionism or passively
acquiesced. But the immobilization of both Jews and Christians
which allowed the determined, single-minded Zionist machine with
its "will-to-deceive" to pursue its injustices and aggressions cannot
be fully understood without acknowledgment of this historic
context. A further ingredient of the mix was the ineffectiveness of
such Arab protests as were made. The Western capital cities where
decisions were made were almost beyond Arab contact, except for
periodic junkets of delegations participating in diplomatic forums
which could not be accused of seeking "open covenants openly
arrived at." Whatever the explanation for Arab failure to make their
case, the average citizen in the West was deprived of first-hand
knowledge about Zionism as the best qualified witnesses—Zionism's victims—might have provided it. A kind of political Darwinism
simply demonstrated the jungle maxim that the fittest survive.

The appropriateness of the description emphasizes the gulf
between this Zionism and the generally recognized purpose of
religion to lift man above the animal instincts and to encourage,
inspire, or goad him to strive for a stature "little lower than the
angels." The contrast also says that the managers of the Zionist
enterprise—the ultimate decison-makers—were little, if any, motivated by *inner* compulsions of the moral absolutes which theologians
attribute to the Divine. There is nothing more absurd in this
Palestinian drama of the absurd than Menachem Begin's claim to all
of Palestine (or even the West Bank) on the grounds of a Divine
promise. It is difficult to find an exonerating historical context to
excuse either Jewish or Christian religionists and theologians for

failing to remind Mr. Begin, the Gush Emunim and the world at large that in typical Zionist practice Mr. Begin is telling—at most—a half truth. For assuming the historic authenticity of the promise to Abraham there was an inseparable, second part. The promise held only as long as the people meticulously and convincingly fulfilled the obligations of the Covenant. Because the ancient kingdoms of Israel and Judah violated the Covenant, God exiled them from the land and encouraged others to ravish it. Even when the eloquent prophet of "the Return"—the anonymous figure we call the Second Isaiah—heralded the return of a people who had not yet completely cleansed its soul, the people were advised the renewed contact between land and people was conditioned by the Divine injunction that the restored Zion was to be a place where God's house would be a "house of prayer for all people." The respectable religionists of the world should be eloquently reminding the sanctimonious Mr. Begin—and the "cowboy" President—that an Israel Defense Force plus American power are no acceptable moral basis for substituting Zionism's tribal, racist, exclusivist, Zionist state for this Divine injunction of universalism.

VII

ZIONISM VS. ANTI-ZIONISM

But in a free society, including Jews who had experienced emancipation and a tradition of anti-Zionism, resistance to Zionism's efforts to set back the clock was inevitable. No one was more conscious of this than the Zionists. The methods employed by the Zionist machine to suppress—or at least to contain—any visible eruptions of anti-Zionism were neither new, nor were they unique to Zionist politics. Herzl's *Diaries* repeatedly record his own doubts about acceptance of his ideas, particularly by Jews in the West; and Weizmann's belated confessions of the inflated Zionist claims of authority at the time of the Balfour Declaration confirm the Zionist management's realization of the synthetic character of their alleged nation. Herzl hurled imprecations at the philanthropic Jews of his days who were committed at least as much as he to improving the life of their less advantaged co-religionists but were not persuaded that emancipation should be so deliberately scuttled in the process. Herzl constantly contrasted the "poor, despised and fine groups of Jews" with "the rich Jews." Jews who disagreed with him were dubbed "smug." To Baron de Hirsch he wrote, not without contempt or at least condescension, "You are the big money Jew, I the Jew of the spirit." It should not be unrecorded that at the same time he asked for 50 million marks to help finance the Zionist project!

But although he was a publicist, Herzl lacked both the means and the technology to escalate his invectives into the kind of verbal *blitzkrieg* which the Zionist machine in the United States was able to produce in the late 30's and early 40's. With Americans generally— and Jews particularly—agitated by guilt over the abominations of Hitler, the Zionist machine at these later dates was eminently more successful, using character assassination, demagoguery, slander, and steamroller size propaganda against even moderate dissidents.

VIII

ANTI-ZIONISM IS "ANTI-SEMITISM"?

The charge of anti-Semite was—and still is—not the least intimidating form of vituperation used by the Zionist *apparat* to stifle opposition. The accusation was—and is—employed against Jews almost as freely as against others.

Two general observations are in order for those who would challenge this tactic. If Zionism is accurately portrayed as the territorial/political ideology it is and if opposition to it is responsible and avoids *ad hominem* argumentation, then in a free society there is no reason to be apologetic or defensive for political opposition to Zionism any more than to any other political movement. Too often opponents of Zionism are inadequately prepared for responsible, documented, supportable opposition. And often, even substantively sound opposition is left vulnerable to diversionary attack as anti-Semitism because the opponent employs some of the stereo-typical language of historic anti-Semitism. Loose talk about "international Jewry" and "conspiracies" should be avoided. Such objectionable short-hand should be replaced by the published, public record of the specifics of Zionist legislation and documented analyses of its ideology. Examined with such critical analysis the record is incongruous enough in terms of contemporary general concepts of liberal, open societies.

The second observation is that wherever possible—and it is possible more often than not—it is important to make emphatically clear the distinction between Judaism and Jew and Zionism and Zionist. The distinction should not be made patronizingly or condescendingly. Personalities and substance should be used to illustrate the asserted difference. Once the separatist and exclu-

sivist character of Zionism is specified as the basis for *political*
opposition many Jews will agree even though they may have been
previously submerged by the flood of Zionist propaganda. It was
less than heroic or omniscient for so many Jews to have been either
coerced or seduced by the sheer bulk and deception of Zionist
propaganda. But such un-heroics were not the monopoly of Jews.
Had they been limited to Jews there would not now exist the
sovereignized version of Zionism which is so responsible for the de-
stabilization of the Middle East. And the process of now separating
the men from the boys—the committed Zionists from the misled
followers—must be an exercise in patience, de-toxification, of
substituting hard, alternative facts and programs for the over-
indulgence in Zionist *hashish*.

IX

SOME PERSONAL ENCOUNTERS

There have, of course, been more corporeal, more physically
punishing techniques of Zionist persuasion. In a long career,
fortunately sustained by an enviable independence for most of life's
necessities, memory recalls many examples. I hesitate to person-
alize. The role of martyr is one I have never coveted, preferring—as
the saying goes—to "give ulcers not contract them." Anonymous
threats to life, my own and that of my wife, unidentified telephone
calls in the middle of the night, social ostracism by groups easy to
take or leave anyway, prescribed defamations by former colleagues
who knew better, the stupid observation that if I were named a
director of the cooperative apartment building in which we lived for
some years no "self-respecting Jew" would ever buy an apartment
in the building, the sheep-herd agreement by both Jewish and other
cooperative owners to the ridiculous proposition, the refusal, on
occasions, of landlords to rent available auditorium space to anti-
Zionists for a meeting, Zionist storm-troopers breaking into a
meeting at Town Hall in New York and disrupting a peaceful
gathering, rescue by some of "New York's finest" from a re-grouped
gang of the same storm-troopers outside the same meeting,
intimidation of book stores that were imprudent enough to display
some of my literary efforts where the public's curiosity might be at
least piqued, canned editorials in the so-called "Jewish" press
about things I was alleged to have done or said without ever
reporting a line about what actually was done or said, nothing but
stone-walling silences in response to efforts to have corrections

made, explanations from the paragon of liberalism, David Susskind, that if he were to give anti-Zionists time on a talk show he once M.C.'d in New York the great philanthropist, Helena Rubinstein, would terminate her lip-stick commercials, elucidation by another paragon of investigative journalism, Mike Wallace, that it was not necessary to give some exposure to the anti-Zionist viewpoint because "everyone knew Elmer Berger's position already." It is a long, repetitive and not very original list of attempted blackmail and suppression or evasion by many of those who are now crying "oil blackmail" and of near-terror by those who are now most eloquently denouncing terrorism. But in the perspective of more than thirty years I think the tormentors have been more tormented than the intended victim. Now, after these more than three decades, I hope to add to their frustration by saying I look upon these episodes with more amusement than anger, though I cannot take an oath I accepted these demonstrations with equanimity at the time.

X

STRANGE ENCOUNTERS
OF THE SECOND PERSON VARIETY

Others, however, were not so fortunately situated. And Zionist efforts at coercion were not limited only to those of us who were attempting to provide leadership. I offer a few examples of these once-removed experiences.

A. RAILROAD TYCOON

There was the Zionist in Kansas City, Missouri who was a grain-broker and a director of the Missouri-Kansas-Texas Railroad. "Katy", as it was called, carried a large part of the cereals shipped from the farmlands of middle America to ports on the Gulf of Mexico. In the war years, railroad cars were at a premium and grains benefited no one and brought no profits to traders if they were not moved from silos and storage-elevators.

A prominent member of the Chicago Board of Trade who specialized in brokering wheat and corn had become an enthusiastic member of The American Council for Judaism [an American Jewish organization that opposed Zionism]. Unlike some other prominent supporters he did not attempt to conceal the association.

Suddenly, our Chicago friend found that the grains he wanted to ship on the "Katy" were assigned a very low priority or given none at all. It took a long fight, enlisting the help of the government which had a vital interest in moving the grains, to bring the problem to the attention of the proper authorities of the railroad and have the "confusions" untangled! The Kansas City Zionist, so far as I know, remained unscathed.

Sometime during this period of encounter between our Chicago friend and the "Katy" I went to Kansas City. A young man there who occupied a junior executive position with the railroad had agreed to organize a council meeting and to serve as the leader for a local Council chapter if there were a sufficient response. I had an appointment with this man in the office of an executive of one of the city's leading department stores. When I arrived, the Zionist railroad director was present. The alert Zionist Gestapo had heard about my planned visit and the young railroad executive's active interest. The Zionist director had informed the young railroad executive that he wished to meet me. The request had been made politely, apparently without hostility. After the usual amenities the Zionist began his campaign. He informed me he had personally met Chaim Weizmann on one of Weizmann's visits to the United States and had traveled with the World Zionist Organization's President as Weizmann attempted to recruit other prominent Jews. And the Kansas City Zionist informed me that he had never heard Weizmann talk about Zionism in terms I used in my lectures or writing. The episode took place a number of years ago and I was a comparative innocent about Zionism myself measured by what I have learned in the intervening years. But I was not so naive to fail to recognize Weizmann's "will-to-deceive". The Zionist Robespierre knew how to give American prospects the "soft-sell".

I tried to explain to this business tycoon that Weizmann had simply employed standard operating procedure for politicians. But in the end neither knowledge nor logic could prevail over the Zionist's economic and political clout in his home city. The more I confronted him with unimpeachable Zionist sources the more infuriated he became. Finally, he forbade the young executive of his railroad to take a leading role in the effort to organize a Council group in Kansas City.

The organizational meetings proceeded with measurable success. Several months later my young friend was transferred from Kansas City to a terminal of the "Katy" in Texas. He continued his support of the Council and his vindictive and uninformed tormentor continued to harass him. Several months after all this the young man committed suicide. Later, I met his sorrowing widow at a Council Annual Conference. She told me unrelieved discouragement over his career opportunities had so depressed her husband that she, at least, had no doubt this played a major role in the tragic decision to take his own life.

B. "FREE" MARKETING

Zionist strong-arm tactics did not always end up quite so dramatically tragic, at least if the anti-Zionists involved were not so directly dependent upon some Zionist commissar. At one point in my early years Grover Magnin of the famous I. Magnin stores in California enlisted in the Council ranks. He,too, was satisfied to have his association public. Magnin was one of the prestige merchandizers of the country. And so Magnin's buying power was a factor to be reckoned with among some of the manufacturers of better women's clothing and accessories.

Once when Grover was coming to New York to buy he advised me in advance and offered to invite some of his suppliers to a luncheon where I would. explain the Council. Probably more because of Magnin's market leverage than my eloquence the meeting was a success. It produced a number of new supporters and some financial assistance. Some weeks later one of the dress manufacturers called and asked if I would do him the favor of visiting him at his Seventh Avenue office. When I arrived he took me back down to the building directory in the first floor lobby. There he showed me that opposite the names of those tenants who had contributed to the United Jewish Appeal the words "UJA Contributor" in gold leaf had been placed. Tenants who had not contributed were, of course, denied the decoration. The embellishment was opposite my host's name. He explained that although he agreed with our view he simply could not stand the heat of refusing to contribute. I was not surprised. The story was familiar. But when we returned to his office he told me that he felt he could not continue as a supporter of The Council. During the few weeks since the Magnin luncheon his suppliers had, with pointed regularity and conformity, called or written him to say they could no longer supply him. One or two had even been candid enough to tell him the reason. And he simply felt he could not jeopardize his life's work and the well-being of his family for a principle in 1946 which, in any event, might not become a reality in the form of a Zionist state.

C. PEER PRESSURES

Not all Zionist strong-arm methods were economic or political. The economic roots of hundreds of thousands of American Jews— perhaps even millions—were not so easily ascertained so the Zionist hit men could cut them. But often the nerve-centers of the family-life of the average American Jew proved not to be beyond the reaches of the ubiquitous and insidious Zionist network. People who surfaced as supporters of the anti-Zionist position, or even as neutralized withholders of support, suddenly found there were no more foursomes for golf. Or, their children were harassed, either at public schools or in religious schools. Or their wives suddenly found they were no longer the necessary fourth at the afternoon bridge game or mahjong session. Rabbis were denied even the opportunity to be candidates for pulpits.

Confirmation that these examples selected from personal experience and the experience of friends and associates are not exceptions was provided in an interesting article by an admitted Zionist in a recent issue of *The Progressive*.[16] The authoress was a member of Breira.[17] She was once asked by a Christian member of a national peace organization, "Why are American Jews so callous to the suffering of the Palestinians?" The writer of the article admits she was "troubled and frightened." Reporting the incident she describes the things she might have told her questioner by way of explaining what the questioner had perceived. And the following— coming from a person who is more pro-Israel perhaps than I—and who was, at one time, closer to the establishment, confirms these personal experiences. This Breira "Zionist" writes:

> I could have told her of the witch hunt tactics and McCarthyite smear campaigns used by the Jewish Establishment to hound Breira out of existence in an effort to conceal the reality of a split in the American Jewish community.
>
> I could have criticized the suppression of free speech in American Jewish institutions—the pressures that prevent dovish or dissident Jews from organizing in synagogues, Jewish community centers, and meetings of major national Jewish organizations. I could have talked further of Jewish attempts to suppress free speech on this issue among non-Jewish American peace groups as well, such as denunciations of the American Friends Service Committee as "anti-Semitic" and "dupes of the Palestine Liberation Organization" for insisting that any true peace must include a viable state for the Palestinians.
>
> I could have told her about a shocking private debate among

American Jews as to whether we can really take the "risk" of genuine open discussion on this issue, and of the agonizing done by staunch leftists—who would champion anyone else's right to free speech—before cautiously deciding for free speech "but with discipline."[18]

None of this explanation was given as answer, however, because the writer of the article confesses

I needed to know whether I could trust her before I could tell her the truth. I did not want to seem to dissociate myself from the collective body of Jews to win her approval. For while I may share some of her views, I share the fate of my fellow Jews.[19]

The writer then admits that this reason is "emotional." A somewhat less emotional explanation for the acquiescence of many Jews may be more generally applicable.

XI

"LET THE PEOPLE KNOW"

It *could* be argued none of these suppressive practices could have been efficacious unless the majority of Jews—and perhaps Christians—were so committed to Zionist principles that they abandoned their loyalties to such American values as political freedom, freedom of speech and assembly and, in general, the right to be different and even dissident. Unfortunately, that is the assumption of entirely too many weary or defeated anti-Zionists, Americans and Arabs, Jews, Christians and Moslems. But it is much too facile an explanation. The ignorance of the media, the mendacity of American politicians, including Presidents, the inadequacy of Arab information, all combined to produce simple peer pressure. It was *thought* that to be an anti-Zionist—and even more a vocal, visible anti-Zionist—was simply not "the thing to do." So the historic tradition of American anti-Zionism was eroded and American Jews could be portrayed as either over-whelmingly in support of, or at least acquiescers in, Zionist policies and ideologies they did not understand because the hucksters of the movement exercised the "will-to-deceive" and there were comparatively few then to say, "No."

I am not here to apologize for these American Jews, and it is too late for any condemnation to be completely effective in undoing the injustices to which they contributed or in exorcising the corruption of their own spiritual heritage to which they were seduced. But their complicity in the evil was not isolated. It was not some limited, "Jewish" phenomenon.

1. Guilt ran—and to the extent Zionism is still an operative factor in American decision-making it still runs—from the White House to the boy who delivers groceries, from the business tycoon who listens to the Anti-Defamation League about the Arab boycott to the applicant for a job, prepared to mute his feelings on this problem for fear that his independent view of Zionism or its Middle East state will deprive him or her of the employment opportunity. Guilt runs also to the Arabs who three decades ago may not have fully understood the complexities of public opinion formation in this democracy, or may have decided they did not have the means to cope with the complexities. But it is difficult today to offer these same apologetics for Arab failure to make clear their alternatives to Zionist manipulation of the Middle East.

2. The blind forces of history are surfacing for Americans— including American Jews—the economic and strategic importance of "the Arabs." But without an energetic and systematic campaign to reinforce these impersonal considerations with greatly increased emphases upon the morality and equality of "the Arabs' " case, these pragmatics are still at the mercy of the Zionist sloganeers who simplistically put the issue as one of "Jews versus oil."

3. Healthy stirrings of conscience among a new generation of emancipated American Jews are increasingly visible within the larger shift of American opinion. They are, understandably, saddled with yet another result of *fait accompli* Zionist diplomacy. From their perspective and what they see as reality the State of Israel is a geo-political fact. They are, therefore, unprepared to accommodate to any formula which might appear to them—perhaps through Zionist misrepresentation of Arab positions—to have as its objective the undoing of this reality. But they have very serious reservations, which they do not conceal, about the Zionist character of the state, its militarism, its violations of human rights, and its arrogance. It is a challenge for all of us long-time observers of the Zionist phenomenon to nourish and cultivate these misgivings and to provide alternatives.

4. And finally, all of us need to remember that despite discou-

ragements, there is no more certain maxim in a democracy than the necessity to "Let the people know." If the Zionists cannot afford to tell the truth because of the anti-democratic character of their fundamental ideology and politics, if the politicians are afraid to tell the truth—assuming they know it—because of their bondage to the slavish stereotype of political reprisal, if the media are still trembling because of the ghosts and contemporary carbon copies of David Susskind's patron, Helena Rubinstein, the country is still free. "The Arabs" today have the resources to exploit this freedom in dignified and responsible ways. They need not choose between an olive branch and the weapons of a freedom fighter, to use Yassir Arafat's eloquent phrase. They can provide both—and the situation calls for both urgently. The greatest ally of evil is still for good men to do nothing, or for the good men who attempt to do something about it to be held on minimal rations when there is no lack of possible nourishment.

At the climax of the Zionist campaign for American support of its state three decades ago, Morris Raphael Cohen, one of the great, liberal American spirits who was also a devoted Jew, said

> Though most of the leaders of Zionism in America are sincerely and profoundly convinced of the compatibility of Zionism and American-ism, they are nonetheless profoundly mistaken. Nationalistic Zionism demands not complete individual liberty for the Jew, but group autonomy.[20]

Nothing has changed the accuracy of this formulation. It explains completely why Zionism has had to operate with deceit, with coercion, with whatever of the tools of totalitarianism it could employ in a fundamentally free society. It explains why in the United States, although it may not have used automatic rifles and rockets, it employed what weapons of terror it could to deprive women, children and bread-winners of the full dignity of free choice.

I may perhaps be forgiven in my veteran years if I say that beyond microscopic examination of the deliberate ambiguities of diploma-cies, beyond the still frustrating shrouds of ignorance woven of either Zionist willfulness or neglect by those who could supply information, I sense something of the resurrection of the Old Testament Prophets and their Judaism (and the Christianity of Jesus) with a soaring spirit which will not be denied. And I continue to believe that if we who have known for so long so much of the truth about these problems continue to hold the standard high we will see the day when

Justice shall flow like water
And righteousness like a mighty stream.
And when no one shall hurt or destroy on
God's Holy Mountain.*

*Extracted from Amos 5:24 and Isaiah 65:25.

NOTES

1. Alexandra U. Johnson. *Israeli Torture of Palestinian Political Prisoners in Jerusalem and the West Bank: Three State Department Reports*. No. 14 in the Public Affairs Series. New York: Americans for Middle East Understanding, Inc. Reprinted from an article in Palestine Human Rights Bulletin, number 17, April 1979.
2. Ludwig Lewisohn, ed., *Theodor Herzl*. Cleveland, Ohio and New York: The World Publishing Co., 1955, p. 233. This book contains the complete text of Herzl's *The Jewish State* and is the source of references made here to the Herzl book.
3. Ibid., p. 235.
4. Ibid., p. 240.
5. Ibid., p. 247.
6. Paul Goodman, ed. *Chaim Weizmann, Tribute in Honor of His Seventieth Birthday*. London: Victor Gollancz Ltd., 1945, p. 147.
7. Ibid., pp. 155–158.
8. Ibid., p. 199.
9. Ibid., pp. 207–208.
10. Ibid., p. 158.
11. George Antonius. *The Arab Awakening*. New York: G. P. Putnam's Sons, 1946, p. 268.
12. Ibid.
13. Wayne Halperin. *The Political World of American Zionism*. Detroit: Wayne University Press, 1961.
14. Ibid., p. 22.
15. Ibid., p. 23.
16. Carolyn Toll. "American Jews and the Middle East Dilemma," *The Progressive*, August 1979, pp. 28ff.
17. An organization of Jews—many of them admitted Zionists—who believed that peace between Israel and "Arabs" was possible only by recognizing the nationality of Palestinians and according them their national rights. They tried to mobilize American support for so-called "doves" in Israel.
18. Toll, op. cit.
19. Ibid.
20. Morris Raphael Cohen. *The Faith of a Liberal*. New York: Henry Holt and Company, 1946, p. 329.

4

Mainline Churches and United States Middle East Policy

Rev. Peter Johnson

1. INTRODUCTION

As a component of the general American ideological and cultural system, religious thought has an impact upon the worldview and perceptions of policy-makers, and thus it makes a contribution to foreign policy formulation. Religion also intervenes as an actor in the formation of foreign policy, particularly through the activity of the churches in missions and in international relief and aid programs. In the case of policy towards the Middle East, the religious overlay is particularly important.

In general in the United States, where Protestant Christianity underlies the dominant ethos, religion has endowed the "American way of life" or the "American system" with sacred characteristics. This usually does not include 100 percent endorsement of particular government policies, but it has meant support for general policy directions and goals, without fundamental questioning of presuppositions. In a second area, religion has usually given support to an overall world-view characterized by racial, ethnic, and religious prejudice. Third, over the past decades, the struggle against communism and its chief proponent, the Soviet Union, has been reinforced by religion. Although these three factors have been altered or attenuated over the past two decades, for most of U. S. history they have played important roles, as religious factors affecting U.S. policy towards what went on outside its own contingent. These factors have helped shape policy towards the Middle East.

In the Middle East, though, several other religious factors are at play. Palestine is "the Holy Land" where the events of the Old Testament took place, and where Jesus lived, was crucified, and was resurrected. Thus for Christians what happens in Palestine is of particular interest. Moreover, Christianity has always regarded Jews in a special manner, and therefore the building of a Jewish state was bound to elicit close regard from Christians. That this attempt took place in "the Holy Land" intensified religious concern.

2. RELIGION AND POLITICS IN THE UNITED STATES

Religion and politics are intimately related in the United States. Despite the constitutional separation of church and state, religious rhetoric has always been used by U.S. politicians, and religious teachings have often guided them. Religion is sometimes used cynically, by presidents and politicians, but it is almost always used. On the other hand, the churches have always sought to have an effect on the body politic, and at many times they have played a crucial role in directing policies.

An interesting example of the close relation between church and state can be seen in the career of John Foster Dulles.[1] The son of a Presbyterian minister and the grandson of a man who served as Secretary of State for eight months in the 1890s, Dulles was motivated to join the public service and deeply imbued with religious training. An international lawyer in the 1920s and 1930s, he attended a meeting of church notables in Oxford, England in 1937. He was struck by the openness of the church leaders to deal with humanity as a whole, and saw this as an element missing in the narrow nationalisms of international affairs. He began to become involved in the work of the Federal Council of Churches in the U.S., and in 1940 he was appointed as head of its Commission for a Just and Durable Peace, which was seeking to find a new order for the world once peace came. The Commission labored under Dulles' influence to project the idea of a new and more effective League of Nations. At first President Roosevelt was cool to the idea, but after Dulles met with him in early 1943 he became more positive. Dulles and the Federal Council were encouraged enough about the possibilities for the United Nations that they began, with other like-minded groups, an intensive campaign of popular support. By the summer of 1944 the Big Powers began, at Dumbarton Oaks, to write the charter for the United Nations Organization. Dulles continued

his activity for the church committee, even while working closely
with the Republican Party, and specifically for New York Governor
Thomas Dewey. His church connections were helpful in keeping
him prominent, so that even after Truman defeated Dewey in the
1948 presidential campaign Dulles was appointed to a position in
the Department of State. He was thus poised for being named, when
the Republicans came to power four years later, as Eisenhower's
Secretary of State. From that position he had a profound effect upon
U.S. policy.

3. THE "MAINLINE" CHURCHES

Of all the many religious organizations in the United States, the
so-called mainline Protestant denominations have been the most
important in contributing to shaping the public ethos. These
churches, Episcopal, Presbyterian, Congregational, and Methodist,
and the inter-church agencies which they dominate, have shaped
the public ethos not because their members are a majority of the
U.S. population but because they are the churches of the upper
class. This is a general statement: there are members who are not
upper class, and there are upper class persons not in those
churches. These churches have been active in education, founding
schools and colleges such as Harvard, Yale, Princeton, Boston
University, and many others. They have maintained large missionary organizations, such as the National Council of Churches and
the World Council of Churches, and thus they have access to and
influence upon many other churches in the United States and
abroad.

Their membership is little more than 25 million, just 10 percent of
the nation's population, yet these are the old churches, representing the descendants of the original religious associations set up by
settlers in the 17th century. These are the churches of the WASP,
the White Anglo-Saxon Protestant. Furthermore, these are the
churches joined by those who climb the ladder of social mobility.
When Eisenhower became President, for example, he joined the
Presbyterian church. To social mobility is added religious mobility,
a phenomenon not found so readily in most other cultures.

This paper will concentrate on the role of the religious mainline
establishment in the formulation of U.S. foreign policy. In so doing it
will leave aside any role that might be played by other substantial
religious groups, such as the Southern Baptists and other Protestant groups whose combined numbers are much larger than the
mainline memberships. We also leave aside the Roman Catholic

Church, which alone counts some 50 million adherents. We do this because of our view of how foreign policy is made in the United States: it is not made by a majority, in any democratic sense, but mainly by members of the upper class, influenced as they are by their own class organizations and their perceptions of what is needed to further their interests. These other non-mainline churches, moreover, have not been organized to affect public policy in international affairs, although the presidency of Jimmy Carter and the upsurge of more conservative Protestant groups, on the one hand, and the obvious role of the Catholic Church in such political movements as the anti-abortion struggle on the other, may presage a new prominence for the voices of such churches. Yet for at least some time in the future, the WASP churches of the establishment, grouped in the National Council of Churches, will continue to play the most important organized religious role in influencing the formulation of foreign policy.

These churches are large organizations, and they are not easily influenced to follow new directions. They move in a slow manner, with many committees, commissions, task forces, and bureaucratic channels. They are rich: the United Presbyterian Foundation, for instance, administers more than a quarter of a billion dollars of church funds on a national level. The United Methodists and the Episcopalians may have more. These churches are influenced by events in the world, but practical changes in policies and orientations are shaped from within. To the extent that the churches have been supportive of Israel over the years, this outcome is largely a result of the close relations which Jewish supporters of Israel maintain with decision-makers at many levels of the churches' structures. On many issues and concerns Jews and Christians work together in important forms of cooperation. So far, religious people with a constituency in the Arab Middle East have not developed similar forms of cooperation with the mainline churches, although increasing efforts have been made in recent years by the newly-formed Middle East Council of Churches. Yet even here, the cooperation tends to be based on a single-issue approach, unlike the multiform cooperation Jews have undertaken with Christians.

Our focus means that we will not examine so-called popular religion, that which is preached in pulpits and taught in Sunday School classes around the country, and which may be believed by members of the church. We will look rather at the leadership sections of the church, which often have opinions and implement policies which are poorly or not fully understood by church members. The leadership sections decide how the churches' money is spent, they train church leaders, and they make the overall policy decisions. They write in the church press. They oversee the missionary activities of the church, which are quite extensive in the Middle East, as we will see.

In the preceding sections we have presented a brief overview of the general influences working on mainline Protestant leaders as they approach policy questions. To their general policy orientations is often added a special relationship with the Middle East, with Middle Easterners, or with people involved in the problem. In succeeding sections we will discuss first of all relations with Jews, which have led some American church leaders to be anti-Zionist and some to be pro-Zionist. Second, we will discuss the influence of the missionaries and the mission establishment, whose approach to the Middle East is influenced by a knowledge of and concern for activities in the Arab world in general. Third, we will look at the church programs for Palestinian refugees which, although close to the missionary concern, have developed their own approach. Fourth, we will examine recent developments in the National Council of Churches. Finally, we will discuss briefly the recent upsurge of interest in the Palestinian cause among some black Christian groups.

4. THE MAINLINE CHURCHES AND JUDAISM

Ever since its founding Christianity has had an ambivalent relation towards Judaism, and hence towards Jews. The Christian religion began within Judaism, and Jesus presented his teaching as a fulfillment of Jewish law. As Christianity spread to people beyond those who were born Jews, or who had converted to Judaism, a question arose about the status of the Jewish people. Was the old covenant religion which God had established with the Jewish people now defunct, replaced by a new covenant made with those who believed in Jesus as the savior? In his Letter to the Romans Paul points out that the Jews are not rejected—the covenant, according to Paul, has been expanded. But Paul begged the question: if Jews are not rejected, just what is their status? The question bedeviled Christians ever after.

In the first centuries of the expansion of Christianity through the Roman Empire, there was considerable competition between the established religion of the Jews who lived in many empire cities and the new Christian movement. In the process of that competition there developed a rather vicious Christian polemic against Jews, while on the other hand the Jewish authorities did all they could to stamp out this imposter religion of the Christians. (An interesting account of this competition is provided in Karl Kautsky's *The Foundations of Christianity*, a work of Marxist social analysis). In the four gospels it can be noted that the later that one was written the more anti-Jewish is the orientation.

Thus for Christians a practical and popular anti-Jewish polemic has tended to co-exist through history with a theological and Biblical recognition of a special relation between Christians and Jews. This antinomy has created the possibility for a wide variety of Christian attitudes and actions. In addition, there have been various social and economic factors defining the relationships between the two groups—perhaps the best treatment of these elements is found in Abram Leon's book on *The Jewish Question: A Marxist Interpretation.*

The Protestant reformation brought to Christianity a new approach to the Bible, which was translated into the vernacular and published for the faithful to read themselves. In America, the triumphalist Protestantism which established itself was undergirded by a strong Biblical theology, which itself was internalized. America was seen as "the promised land," the settlers as the Israelites escaping from the bondage of their taskmasters in the old world, the native Americans as the Canaanites whose extermination was a theological and practical necessity, the covenant forms of government set up here as reflections of the rule of law established with the Ten Commandments and the Mosaic law, and more. More strongly than in the earlier periods of Christian history Old Testament themes came to the forefront in American Protestantism, and with them a sympathy for the Old Testament religion, and thus for Judaism and the Jews. If this was emphasized among white Protestants, it was particularly strong among Blacks who read the Bible. The blacks in slavery, and later on, compared themselves with the Hebrew slaves in Egypt, singing in their spirituals:

> When Israel was in Egypt's land,
> Let my people go.
> Oppressed so hard they could not stand
> Let my people go.
> Go down, Moses, way down in Egypt land,
> Tell Old Pharaoh, let my people go.

Before Zionism was elaborated as a political movement there were many Christians who wished, romantically, for a "restoration of the Jews to their land." (Nahum Sokolow's *History of Zionism* has an extensive treatment of British Christian Zionism, as a comparison). Typical of early nineteenth century feelings in this regard is the following statement made by President John Adams in 1818, sometime after he left office:

> I really wish the Jews again in Judea, an independent Nation, for, as I believe, the most enlightened men of it have participated in the amelioration of the philosophy of the age; once restored to an independent government, and no longer persecuted, they would soon wear away some of the asperities and peculiarities of their character. I wish your nation may be admitted to all the privileges of citizens in every part of the world. This country [the United States] has done much; I wish it may do more, and annul every narrow idea in religion, government and commerce.[2]

Note that this idea of "restoration" comes with a less favorable attitude towards Jews, or some Jews, who have "asperities and peculiarities" of character. For Adams, the solution is an independent government and an end to persecution; he wishes for a full extension of bourgeois freedoms to Jews and thinks an independent state might help facilitate the process. This point of view is perfectly compatible with Zionism, which included as a basic premise that the "asperities and peculiarities" of Jewish character were a result of their status as a nation without a nation-state.

Another trend in the United States, on the other hand, started from the same "asperities and peculiarities" and proposed that the desired "wearing away" of these character traits would come through assimilation into the ambient culture. Such assimilation was quintessentially available, it was thought, in the bourgeois democracies—Adams has already pointed to what America has done. Among the mainline Protestant churches the most noted voice for this perspective was *The Christian Century*, an independent Protestant magazine which represents mainline Protestantism as well as any other publication. (Hertzel Fishman has done a rather superficial analysis of *The Christian Century* in his study, *American Protestantism and a Jewish State*[3].) The magazine upheld the theory of the United States as a melting pot, and was opposed to any Jews who resisted "melting" into the American culture. Thus during the Thirties and Forties the magazine was consistently opposed to Zionism.

Conjoined with the "melting pot" liberal approach as an upderpinning for anti-Zionism, many authors in *The Christian Century* were bothered by the continuing existence, and now particularly the self-assertiveness, of the Jewish people as a people. For many Christian theologians the existence of this people was somewhat of an epiphenomenon. If Christianity is indeed the fulfillment of the Old Testament Law, then despite Paul's statements in Romans the Jewish people should fade away. According to this theological understanding, it is the covenant with God which originally created the Jewish people, and which held them together. But since that covenant has changed since the arrival of Jesus Christ, how can one explain the persistence of the Jewish people? Within Christian circles, many liberals prior to World War II held that liberal democracies promised the kind of "integration" that was needed to finally end the special peoplehood. For conservative Christians, it was thought, on the basis of certain New Testament prophecies, that a return of the Jewish people to the Holy Land was a necessary prelude to their conversion to Christianity, which was a necessary prelude to the coming of the Kingdom of God. These folks supported Zionism, then, not as a way for the fulfillment of Judaism in the terms that Jews understood it, but rather for the fulfillment of the Christian goal of the conversion of the Jews.

Close to the liberal point of view, and often part of it, was an approach that upheld Judaism as a religion, spiritual like other religions, the property of the individual and his conscience, but not constitutive of any special status. This approach played down any nationalist understandings of "peoplehood." Elmer Berger has been a distinguished spokesman for this point of view, along with others in the American Council for Judaism and successor organizations. But Elmer Berger speaks from within the Jewish faith. There are many non-Jews who will tell Jews what their religion really is, from outside the faith, a position that I find presumptuous and even arrogant.

There were of course many in the establishment who developed and have maintained pro-Zionist points of view. Some did this for theological reasons, but many did it for cultural or political reasons. I mentioned above the close ties of cooperation which many Christians have with American Jewish supporters of Zionism and Israel. In the absence of countervailing forces of equal strength, it seems quite natural for these Christians to support Israel, in what I call "cultural" support. Many members of the famous Christian Council for Palestine, or its successor the American Christian Palestine Committee founded in 1945, were cultural supporters of Zionism, at a time when sympathy for the Jews was at a crest following revelations of the Nazi slaughter of millions of Jews and the still unresolved problem of many thousands of Jewish refugees.

Thus thousands of Christians were pleased to sign statements of support for the Zionist cause and to participate in conferences and meetings.

Reinhold Niebuhr, the noted theologian and ethicist, was both a cultural and a political supporter of Zionism. He polemicized against Christian anti-Zionists, not so much on theological grounds as on grounds of "realism." Realism was the hallmark of his ethical method. He inveighed against the liberal tendency to recognize only the rights of individuals and deny the rights of collectivities of humans. The Jews, Niebuhr stated, *needed* a state, a place to go they could call their own. In an earlier period he would have settled for a place other than Palestine,[4] but the events of the 1940s made him a strong backer for Palestine.

Niebuhr was vice-president of the Socialist Party in the United States, and as such he was closely tied to scores of Jewish militants in the trade unions and working class movements. It was his alliance with these people as much as anything that led to his support of Zionism. It is noteworthy, and calls for ongoing reflection, that often the progressive forces in a particular country were more likely to espouse the Zionist cause, while the more conservative were quicker to support Arab interests.

5. THE MAINLINE CHURCHES AND MISSIONS IN THE MIDDLE EAST

The first American missionaries went to the Middle East in the first quarter of the 19th century, intent upon evangelization of Muslims. It did not take them long to appreciate the difficulty of such a task, and they soon changed their emphasis to that of "renewing" the ancient churches of that area. Gradually that emphasis too became eclipsed by a focus on service, the Christian principle of serving others, following the Golden Rule of "love your neighbor as yourself." The other emphases remained, but the major commitment of missionary time, money, and personnel became health and education. In the 1850s was founded in Beirut a missionary printing press, with the permission of the Ottoman authorities. Initially oriented towards reproductions of the Scriptures in Arabic, this press soon launched into other Arabic material, providing a valuable source for Arabic literature in a culture dominated by Turkish influence and attitudes. Most notable among the American institutions so founded is the American University of Beirut, begun in the 1860s as the Syrian Protestant College. Other well-known institutions are Robert College in Istanbul and the American

University in Cairo. These institutions of higher education were backed up by a host of preparatory schools, including schools for girls which played a special role in educating women to the Western modes of thought and comportment deemed so important by the missionaries, husbands and wives. None of these institutions was very successful in converting people to Protestant Christianity, but they played a key role in educating an emerging bourgeoisie in Western thought and methods, while inculcating within them a respect for the United States.

During the first one hundred years of American missionary activity, United States foreign policy had little interest in the Middle East. With the exception of a few consular and commercial representatives, there was no attention paid to this part of the world. Not until World War One was well under way that the first American intelligence agent was appointed to the Middle East, based in Cairo. William Yale, who took up this post, had a few years previous experience in the area with Standard Oil.

Until that time, information about the Middle East was conveyed to officials and the general public alike by travelers (mainly pilgrims to the Holy Land) and by missionaries. Notable among the travelers was Mark Twain, whose *Innocents Abroad* records some of the crassest racist stereo-types about Middle Easterners. Edward Said has presented some of the missionary and Orientalist approaches in his book on *Orientalism*, and Basim Musallam has added some missionary ingredients in his review of Said's book published in *MERIP Reports* in 1979. Musallam looks at some of the writings of Henry Jessup, books such as *Syrian Home Life* and *The Women of the Arabs*, published for an American audience. Certainly Jessup's books had an influence on American opinions, as did the numerous sermons and speeches delivered by returning missionaries in fund-raising tours in churches around the nation. One can easily visualize the effects of the lurid descriptions of Arab morals and mores—good American Christian people would give more support to the valiant "civilizing" and Christianizing work of the missionaries.

If it was in the interest of the nineteenth century missionaries to portray the Arabs with "unspeakable slander, prejudice and intolerance," to borrow a quote cited by Musallam, the increase of American official interest in the Middle East in the early twentieth century called for a different approach. The defeat of the Ottomans in World War One led to the question about the disposition of their empire. Combined with this issue was the fact of the discovery of oil in the Middle East. The United States worked heroically to ensure an

"Open Door policy" for U.S. companies in a region where British, French, and Dutch companies had pre-eminence. The questions of oil and the political status of Arab lands have remained as key and interrelated factors in the determination of U.S. policy towards the area ever since. But at this moment oil was only a background concern.

There was a more general concern, in the period just after the First World War, for the political status of the Arab lands, and more precisely for ensuring a political status which would guarantee American economic and cultural access to the area. Missionaries were active in campaigning for approaches to the "Eastern Question" which would be favorable to their interests. To the U.S. Inquiry Group set up to determine U.S. policy at the Paris Peace Conference, the head of Near East Missions, Dr. James Barton from Boston, made a proposal for a Federation of Middle East states:

> Behind its elaborate framework of state mechanics was a project for the economic control of the whole of the Near East by a single *protector* which, he hoped, would be the United States working jointly with a great spiritual and educational force, the missionaries of the Near East, whose civilizing influence had already proved its worth.... The whole Near East area was to be kept intact, he argued, because any subdivision into spheres of influence would retard its development.... [The] responsible power would send in a Governor General and other officials from among its own nationals.

> At Paris this American Protestant missionary element was not only Zionism's most influential competitor among the American delegates; at one point it even became the rallying point for anti-Zionist American Jews such as Morgenthau.[5]

The publication of the Weizmann-Feisal correspondence in early January, 1919 represented a high point for Zionist diplomacy. A reaction was not long in coming from the Middle East and from anti-Zionists elsewhere. Missionaries were a key force in what Zionist historian Frank Manuel calls "the most potent single force whittling down the maximalist program of a Jewish Homeland at the Paris Peace Conference."[6]

Professor Westermann of Cornell was head of the Western Asia Intelligence Section of the American Commission at Paris, an outgrowth of the Inquiry. Westermann picked up on a proposal made by Dr. Howard Bliss, president of the Syrian Protestant College in Beirut, and doubtless the most influential American in the Middle East. Bliss had suggested a mixed allied commission to investigate the desires of the Syrians, and by the end of January he

expanded upon what he thought they would find: "a universal desire
for a united Syria, to include Palestine, under an American
protectorate."[7] Bliss, like other members of the faculty of the college
in Beirut, was opposed to French influence in the area, and he had
worked against Jesuit activity for some time. Bliss and others used
Wilson's enunciation of principles of self-determination, seeing it as
a tool against possible French (or British) takeover in the area.

The Bliss initiative was not successful, although it led to the
dispatch of the King-Crane Commission to Syria and Palestine.
That commission accurately read the feelings of the Syro-Palestin-
ian population, at least with regard to the Jewish homeland
question, yet it was not successful in countering the combination of
William Yale's pro-Zionist proposal, the Zionist influence, and most
particularly the concern of Britain and France to control the Middle
East. The missionaries fell back to protecting what they could and
they lobbied the U.S. government to seek accords with Britain and
France which would protect missionary institutions.

From this point on the missionaries were less able to dissemble,
as Henry Jessup had done, telling the Arabs one thing about Arab
culture and telling Americans something else. Although some of
that went on (and probably still does), the missionaries were
increasingly to become "more Arab than thou" as the Palestine
question became a central issue in Arab national politics. The
missionaries were intent upon protecting their own position as
Americans in the Arab world. They were concerned to project an
image of Arabs as a nation committed to its own development, open
to the liberalizing influence of the missions and their institutions,
and increasingly prepared for responsible self-government. Going
the other direction, the missionaries were interested in projecting to
their Arab audiences the most liberal image of America, and it is safe
to say that with many nationalist intellectuals the missionaries were
successful in instilling a view of the general benevolence of the
United States and its institutions and aims which still has not been
shaken. Another word on this subject later.

The missionary influence upon the churches in the United States
remained strong, and it continues to this day to have adherents in
the highest circles of the establishment churches. What we have
here is what might even be called the religious face of the State
Department, which is noted for its pro-Arab cast. The children of
many missionaries have gone into the State Department, serving in
key posts throughout the Middle East. This is particularly true of
educational institutions, by this time free of their church connections. A notable example is President Kennedy's ambassador to

Egypt, John Badeau, formerly president of the American University in Cairo.

In general this group has been pro-Arab, anti-Zionist, anti-communist and of course pro-United States.

In the tumultuous post-World War Two period in the United States, when the U.S. as the great victor of the war and suddenly the world's greatest power was making its decisions about the Palestine question, the missionary influence continued to be felt through the establishment. The counterpart to the Zionist propaganda effort during this period was the Institute of Arab-American Affairs, founded by Arab-Americans, and supported by the Arab League (according to Manuel).[8] A Professor Lybyer, of Robert College in Istanbul, who had served as part of the technical staff for the King-Crane Commission, was associated with the Institute. Philip Hitti of Princeton respresented the Institute as the first Arab witness before the Anglo-American Committee of Inquiry in 1946.

Several important figures with missionary connections were on the Executive Committee of another anti-Zionist organization, the Committee for Justice and Peace in the Holy Land, founded in early 1948 in an almost successful attempt to bring the United States to support reconsideration of the partition decision made by the United Nations in 1947. Reverend Daniel Bliss of Connecticut, grandson of his missionary namesake, was a member. So was Bayard Dodge, president of the American University of Beirut. Other Executive Committee members were Harry Emerson Fosdick of Riverside Church (associated prominently with the Rockefellers); Paul Hutchinson, editor of *The Christian Century* (a Protestant magazine hostile to Zionism); and Gloria Wysner, from the International Missionary Council in the United States. The Executive Director of this interesting organization, which was to continue in existence for only a few years, was Kermit Roosevelt, known a few years later as a C.I.A. agent intimately involved with the overthrow of Mossadegh in 1953, and also as one who worked with Nasser. Roosevelt became vice-president of Gulf Oil in 1958.[9]

We mentioned earlier that one of the goals of the missionaries was to present a strong and effective image of the United States, and Christianity, as a counter to the Soviet Union and Communism, and to Islam as well. After the overt and manifest U.S. government support for the creation of the state of Israel, and for its continued defense, it became more difficult for the missionaries to present the United States in a favorable light. Or rather let us say that the missionaries needed to find some explanation for the anti-Arab direction of their government's policy. Here intervenes the theory of the strength of the Zionist lobby and of its control of the thinking of Americans through the media, through the Jewish vote, through banks and investment firms, and so on. According to this theory and approach, the United States is inherently good, which means inherently pro-Arab in this case, and the best explanation of its anti-Arab policies is its naive subservience to the Zionist propaganda machine. Although we do not want to minimize the strength of the Zionist propaganda effort, we feel this approach is based upon an erroneous understanding of how the United States makes foreign policy, and who makes it. This approach, though, has led to the creation of organizations such as Americans for Middle East Understanding, Americans for Justice in the Middle East, and even American Friends of the Middle East, which have played a role as "counter-lobby" to the Zionist lobby but which fail to touch the real strings of foreign policy decison-making in a society dominated by multi-national corporations. In many of these counter-lobby organizations missionaries have played a role, often an important one.

We can foresee that as the limitations of United States support of Israel become more apparent, the approach of the missionaries will become more widespread, in the mainline churches and without. The missionaries who have for years felt they were crying in a wilderness when speaking in churches in this country will find more persons ready to hear. Already in the political arena we have seen an unheard-of development in this direction, as a presidential aspirant such as John Connally enunciates his position on the Middle East.

These pro-United States, pro-Arab anti-Zionists have a tendency to use the cause of the Palestinians to the extent that it is necessary for them in their overall approach to the Arab world in general, but their political orientation makes them uncomfortable with the Palestine Liberation Organization, and certainly with its more progressive sectors.Indeed, these people are clearly more anti-Israeli than they are pro-PLO. But what does it mean to support the Palestinians without supporting the PLO? There is one section of the church, though, which is much closer to the Palestinian cause, and that is composed of those who have worked with Palestinians through the church programs for refugee work.

6. THE MAINLINE CHURCHES
AND THE PALESTINE REFUGEE PROBLEM

Church World Service, an American church relief organization which later became a part of the National Council of Churches, sent its first aid shipment to Palestine refugees in July 1948. It encouraged interested Americans in Jerusalem to work with Palestinians and expatriate church groups to help Palestinian refugees wherever they were. Soon committees were operating in East Jordan, Lebanon, Syria, the Gaza Strip, and within Israel itself. Church World Service began an appeal for funds and material aid, which were soon being channeled to the International Christian Committees through the Presbyterian Mission office in Beirut and through the United Missionary Council of Palestine and Syria, also based in Beirut. Thus began what has become an important element in the relations of mainline churches to the Middle East.

In 1951 the World Council of Churches, which had been rapidly brought into the Palestine refugee situation, convened a "Conference on Arab Refugee Problems" in Beirut. The World Council had begun its Refugee Division because of concern for Jewish refugees following World War Two, and much of the administrative concern was now turned to the Palestinians. The 1951 conference was attended by 73 delegates and observers, of whom only 19 were Middle Easterners (14 Orthodox and 5 Evangelical). Of the 54 Westerners all but 2 were Americans; and of the 54, 31 lived in the Middle East. This conference, according to its reports, set up structures to facilitate relief, inter-church aid, special projects, publicity, and international conciliation. In the conference statement the participants said, "We are convinced that there can be no permanent settlement of the problem of the Palestinian refugees until there is a settlement of the outstanding political differences between the Arab states and Israel."[10] As part of the settlement, the conference saw the need for a return of some refugees and a general plan of compensation (for all who had lost property). Finally:

> while we recognize the basic right of all refugees to their own homes and property, nevertheless a careful appraisal of the total situation has compelled us to conclude, however, that many Palestinian refugees will have to settle in new homes. For their integration into the life and economy of the Arab States, large sums of money will be needed, and needed quickly.[11]

According to Dr. Elfan Rees, the World Council delegate who wrote the Foreword to the Conference's *Report from Beirut*,

> the delegates were shocked by the deep-seated hatred which the refugees manifest and even nurture against those western nations

whom they hold responsible for their plight and against, a dangerously personalized, United Nations for its failure to do justice and remedy the situation. It was also manifest that the very general and serious deterioration in morale amongst the refugees was driving them to extreme forms of political radicalism. Moreover, involved in these attitudes, was the other fact that the refugees and their leaders were so preoccupied with the recognition of their undoubted rights, in abstract justice, to restitution and repatriation, that they ignored the practical and political obstacles to such a course and refused to contemplate any alternative solutions to their problem which accorded more with the hard facts of the present Near East situation.[12]

The "extreme forms of political radicalism" to which Rees referred were outlined more explicitly by other conference delegates. Edwin Moll from the Lutheran World Federation said, "There is an ideal soil being created for the seeds of communism, and by that I mean *practical* communism because I don't think that the Arabs or [sic] any of the native religions will embrace Marxism."[13] "Christianity," Moll stressed, "has lost appallingly."[14] Dr. Alford Carleton, president of Aleppo College, a mission institution, said that he felt "most deeply . . . the loss of the prestige and power of the U.S. as an impartial and friendly power."[15]

Five years later the World Council of Churches convened another Beirut conference on "The Problem of the Arab Refugees from Palestine." The 1951 conference had acknowledged the political problems preventing a rapid settlement of the refugee problem,it but had set about a fairly traditional refugee relief and resettlement program. By 1956 the focus shifted somewhat. The refugee program had grown substantially in a few years. Over $1 million was channeled in 1954 through the Near East Christian Council, and almost $2 million went through Lutheran sources. By 1955 the total value of church-originated goods and services to the Palestinian refugees exceeded $8 million, a small sum in relation to the need, but still almost a third the size of the United Nations Relief and Works Agency (UNRWA) budget for the same year.

The 1956 conference heard Charles Malik speak on "The Political Realities of the Middle East" and emphasize both at the beginning and the end of his speech that "the Communist penetration of the Near East is very serious."[16] The conference called upon Israel to take the first steps towards a political solution: "The people and government of Israel," according to the Statement; "will find their position in the Middle East more acceptable and their expressed desire for peace more convincing if they take the lead in the process."[17]

We repeat that political measures hold the key to meeting the human problem. Therefore, this Conference is convinced that the churches throughout the world have a threefold duty. They must acquaint themselves thoroughly with the facts and make them as widely known as possible. They must insist that governments redouble their efforts to contribute to a just political solution. With equal urgency, they must appeal to governments and to all Christian people to provide adequate funds for the needs of the refugees.[18]

The refugee program at this time was almost completely suppor- ported by money from U.S. churches. An effort was made to increase the base of support: Oxfam (Oxford Famine Relief, originally British and later international) came in during the 1950s, and by the mid-1960s significant support was coming from church sources in Britain, Germany, the Netherlands, Canada, and the Scandinavian countries.

The 1967 war, with its radical alteration of the situation facing the Palestinian people, led to the convening of another World Council of Churches "Consultation on the Palestine Refugee Problem" in the early fall of 1969. At this Consultation, of 108 participants more than half were Middle Easterners, quite different from the earlier meetings. There were 25 Palestinians present. The non-Middle Eastern delegates represented many countries—certainly Ameri- cans no longer dominated. The Consultation was co-convened by Orthodox and Oriental Orthodox churches, members of the World Council of Churches, but not members of the Near East Council of Churches (NECC). The NECC at that time was made up almost entirely of Evangelical (Protestant) churches, and most of the clergy on area committees were Anglicans (Episcopalians). The Consultation led to a new structure for the refugee work, giving general supervision to a new committee on which Orthodox had full participation and which was independent of the Protestant-domi- nated Near East Council of Churches. (The new refugee committee, by the way, helped along a process which was finally completed in 1974, whereby Orthodox and other churches joined with Protestant [ex-missionary] churches to form the Middle East Council of Churches. Is this the renewal of the ancient churches for which the first missionaries hoped? If so, how different from what they expected.)

The Consultation published a report called *The Palestine Refu- gees—Aid with Justice.* Along with renewed commitment to vocational programs and self-help efforts, the Consultation set up an information bureau to bring out material on "Palestinian refugees and other displaced persons, and the grave injustices done to the Palestinian people."[19] By now, the view of the political nature of the "problem" as a question of justice for a people was deeply shared by the Consultation's participants. They stressed, moreover, "the reality of a Palestinian community, and manifestation of this identity as shown, for example, in the Palestine liberation movement. Awareness of this Palestinian identity may be a first step towards the redress of the injustices done to the Palestinians. This means specifically that all of our work, both in humanitarian fields and in the preparation of educational and informational material, must be done not *for* the Palestinians but *with* them."[20] The Consultation also decided to give particular attention to the special needs of the people in the occupied territories. Finally, the Consultation called for a special appeal for $2 million.

The focus on refugee work came to place less emphasis on relief and more on building and strengthening the Palestinian community(ies) in the various areas where work was going on. In the occupied territories the goal of training and self-help programs, such as loans for small businesses and community development projects, was to provide employment for Palestinians within the occupied territories. Implicit in this emphasis was a recognition that for the sake of the Palestinian community it was important to do what was possible to prevent the increasing reliance upon Israel and the Israeli economy for employment and goods. As Richard Butler, present director of the Middle East and Europe Office of the National Council of Churches, and director of the Palestine refugee program in Jerusalem from 1962-1967 and in Geneva from 1967-1972, put it recently, "The refugee programs have helped keep Palestinians alive and *in place.*"[21]

Twenty-eight percent of the refugee program's 1978 budget was spent on health (mainly for mothers and children), 25 percent on employment opportunities, 15 percent on community development, and 13 percent on educational opportunities.[22] The U.S. churches through Church World Service contributed about $300,000 in cash, a figure which has remained fairly constant, but they also offer clothing and have contributed services which bring that sum up to a contribution of about $1 million. A typical program, supported entirely by the United Methodist Committee on Relief, worked with farmers in the Hebron area to make better use of waste land by planting trees. According to the 1978 report:

> The program gave excellent results. It did not only help the few farmers with whom we worked, but it motivated others to copy its patterns, which be seen [sic] of the fact that in 1978, a total of 80,000

olive seedlings were planted in the Hebron area. This brings the total
of olive trees in this area to about 600,000, whereas the total in 1969
was 150,000 only.[23]

In the face of the occupying government's determination to shape
West Bank agriculture towards its own purposes, and given the
wholesale cutting down of olive trees which occurred in conquered
territories following the 1948–49 war, and especially since olive
trees take seven years to bear after planting, the political significance of this program seems clear. In general, the employees of the
refugee programs attempt as much as is possible to maintain an
attitude of non-cooperation with the Israeli authorities in the West
Bank and in Gaza.

At present, the orientation of the mainline churches at the level of
their official statements is one of support for Palestinian national
aspirations, at least in some form. Certainly the growing thrust of
the refugee program to support political solutions for the "problem," and to see indeed that it is much more than a "refugee
problem," has had its impact upon the mainline churches in the
United States and Europe. We can observe this shift somewhat in
the trends within the National Council of Churches, where it is
significant that the head of the Middle East Office is a person with
long-standing relations with Palestinians.

7. RECENT TRENDS
IN THE NATIONAL COUNCIL OF CHURCHES

Long allies in the civil rights movements and a host of other
progressive reform activities, Jewish organizations and mainline
churches reacted differently to the events surrounding the war of
June 1967. For the Jews, Arab threats before the war promised
calamity; for the Christians, there was not that sense of univocal
alarm. Once the war was over, Jews rallied to Israel more strongly
than before, now that it had "proved itself." Support for Israel
became somewhat of a litmus test, on the part of the Jews, for
continuing good relations with Christian groups. The Christian
groups, though, took a more balanced position.

Shortly after the war the National Council of Churches Executive
Committee came out with a statement similar to what eventually
became United Nations Security Council Resolution 242, adopted

on November 22, 1967, urging Israeli withdrawal from occupied lands, insisting upon Arab recognition of Israel, and calling for a just solution to the Palestine refugee problem. We have spoken earlier of the missionary connection in the mainline churches. It is interesting to note that an important role was played in the formulation of this statement by Alford Carleton, who was at that time a top official in the United Church of Christ. Carleton had been president of Aleppo College. The staff of the National Council's Middle East Office was Harry Dorman, a great-grandson of the first Daniel Bliss, and born in the Middle East himself. Dorman had been secretary for the Near East Christian Council/Council of Churches (the Near East Christian Council became the Near East Council of Churches when the Orthodox church joined it). Also serving with the statement committee as a consultant was the United Presbyterian Middle East representative, Park Johnson, who had lived in the Middle East for the previous seventeen years and was the author of a book on the Middle East and mission strategy called *Middle East Pilgrimage*, published in 1958 by the National Council of Churches as a study book. These missionary representatives were instrumental in changing the orientation of the drafting committee, which had originally been to place the statement about Arab recognition prior to the one about Israeli withdrawal. In its final form the admonition to Israel came first.

In 1969, in a major policy statement *On the Crisis in the Middle East*, the General Board of the National Council of Churches continued the orientation of the 1967 Executive Committee. This document stated:

In the situation of the past twenty years and more, two specific human needs have arisen, continued and remain unsolved.

a) One is the need of the Palestinian Arabs affected by the establishment of Israel, of whom now approximately 1,500,000 are refugees, for a home that is acceptable to them, and for a future in which they discern justice, security and hope. What will constitute a "home acceptable to them" must now be a matter of negotiation in which generosity will be required of many, and compromise by all who are directly involved.

b) The other specific need is security for the Jews in the area. The Jews in the Arab countries of the Middle East and the Jews of Israel must be assured of safety and of their rights. Without this assurance, there will be no justice and peace in the Middle East.[24]

Whereas in 1969 the document referred to "a growing sense of identity among Palestinian Arabs," the emphasis was still on the refugee status. By 1974, though, the focus changed, as evident in the Executive Committee resolution passed in December:

> We call upon Israel and the Palestinians to recognize the right of the other party to the same self-determination which they desire for themselves. We affirm the right of Israel to exist as a free nation within secure borders. We equally affirm the right of the Palestinian people to self-determination and a national entity. . . . Furthermore, we call upon the United States to develop more open contacts within the leadership of the Palestinians, including the Palestine Liberation Organization, as a means of furthering prospects for peace.[25]

After the September 1978 Camp David agreement between Egypt, Israel, and the United States, the Executive Committee pointed to the indispensable need:

> to broaden the context of the peace discussions to include the recognized representatives of the Palestinian people in order to enable them to become full partners in the peace process.[26]

Finally, following the resignation of Andrew Young from the United Nations Ambassadorship in the summer of 1979, the Executive Committee stated on Sept. 7 that "We find ourselves in fundamental agreement with remarks [Young] made to his U.N. Security Council colleagues on August 24, 1979."[27]

It is fair to say that the National Council of Churches, in its statements, has consistently been several years ahead of the U.S. government and public opinion in advocating new approaches and understandings of the Arab-Israeli conflict, the Palestinians, and Israel. Although there are many in the churches who maintain and wish to increase contact and cooperation with Jewish groups, and many who are pro-Israeli, this has not prevented the enunciation of an "even-handed" approach over the past decade. This is not particularly remarkable in itself, but it is noteworthy when put in the context of popular American and popular American Christian attitudes towards Israel, the Palestinians, and the conflict in the Middle East.

Can we ever expect the churches to be more than the liberal stalking horse for the U.S. government? It used to be considered rather "leftist" to call for a recognition of the Palestine Liberation Organization, but is that really "leftist?" The churches have already done that. They have, though, called for certain approaches in the

Middle East which, if honored, would be progressive. Their ties to Middle Eastern churches, their participation with Palestinians in the refugee programs, their participation in world ecumenical bodies in which Third World churches have a majority of votes if not of money, have led to a significant new responsibility for the churches, even the established ones, to act in a more progressive manner, both as they act in world affairs and as they inform the ideology and public ethos in the United States. For those who have a progressive viewpoint on world affairs, or upon the struggle of the Palestinians for the realization of their national rights, participating in the structures of the churches to move them in progressive directions is a worthy engagement.

8. BLACK CHRISTIANS AND THE PALESTINIANS

I would be remiss if I were to ignore the most remarkable, or most remarked-upon, recent manifestation of Christian support for the Palestinian cause, shown by the statements of Black Christian leaders in behalf of the Palestinians, and especially in the visits to the Middle East of both a delegation led by Joseph Lowery of the Southern Christian Leadership Conference and a group from PUSH (People United to Save Humanity) led by Jesse Jackson.

As we mentioned earlier, the Christianity of the Black community has always had a strong component of identification between the people of Israel (in the Bible) and the Black people in America. For religious folk, nurtured in the language of the Scriptures, the return of Jews to Israel after centuries of persecution is a religious event to be celebrated, certainly one to be supported.

Religion plays a stronger role in the Black communities than it does in most other communities in America, and Black preachers are often the most influential men in their communities. For a long period of time there has been an alliance between Black leaders and Jewish leaders on civil rights issues which the two groups had in common. This alliance extended to Black support for the state of Israel. Recently, however, the rate of development of the Black and Jewish communities has led to a division between the two allies, as each group works out its increasingly different agenda. In the case of support of the state of Israel, this has meant that some Black leaders now perceive it as more in their interest to develop alliances with the Afro-Asian bloc overseas than to struggle to maintain the alliance with Jews at home. Reasons for this are complex and do not necessarily mean that suddenly the Palestinian national cause has

been understood. Working behind these recent events are a Third
Worldist ideology, a considerable sympathy for Palestinians and
the violation of their civil rights, the frayed nature of the alliance with
Jews around issues such as the Bakke case (which challenged the
legality of affirmative action), some demagoguery, and a sad
measure of response to the kind of anti-Semitism in the Black
communities which is used to blame the poverty of those areas on
Jewish landlords and shopkeepers rather than on the capitalist
system itself.

It should be noted that most, if not all, of the Black leaders who
have recently achieved notoriety for their positions on the side of
the Palestine Liberation Organization, or at least favoring it, are
devoted to the capitalist system and indeed are intent upon finding
ways to reform it to accommodate Blacks (or, in the case of
Jackson, reforming Blacks to accommodate them to the capitalist
system). Andrew Young himself has been one of the most
sophisticated advocates of the "neocolonial road to development"
as he has worked with Third World leaders through his U.N. post
and shepherded Black American businessmen on tours looking for
investment opportunities in Africa. Andrew Young, interestingly
enough, is not a minister in one of the historic Black churches, but
rather in the United Church of Christ, one of the mainline churches.
And his liberal, somewhat pro-Arab, somewhat anti-Zionist, certainly anti-communist, and definitely pro-United States stance is
typical of the position of many of the leaders of the mainline
churches.

NOTES

(See Bibliography for full entries.)

1. Hoopes, pp. 50–53.
2. Fink, p. 20.
3. Fishman.
4. Interview with Ronald Stone.
5. Manuel, p. 214f.
6. *Ibid.*, p. 223.
7. *Ibid.*, p. 224.
8. *Ibid.*, p. 241.
9. Stork, p. 54.

Johnson

10. World Council of Churches, May 4-8, 1951, p. 44.
11. *Ibid.*.
12. *Ibid.*, p. 5.
13. *Ibid.*, p. 26.
14. *Ibid.*, p. 27.
15. *Ibid.*, p. 17.
16. World Council of Churches, May 21-25, 1956, p. 25.
17. *Ibid.*, p. 10.
18. *Ibid.*, p. 11.
19. World Council of Churches, September 29-October 4, 1969, p. 14.
20. *Ibid.*, pp. 12-13.
21. Interview with Richard Butler.
22. The Middle East Council of Churches.
23. *Ibid.*, p. 25.
24. National Council of Churches, May 2, 1969.
25. National Council of Churches, December 13, 1974.
26. National Council of Churches, 1978.
27. National Council of Churches, 1979.

BIBLIOGRAPHY

American Christian Palestine Committee, *Problems of the Middle East* (Proceedings of a Conference held at New York University, June 5-6, 1947). New York: A.C.P. c., 1947.

Butler, Richard, Director, Middle East and Europe, National Council of Churches. Personal interview.

Clemens, Samuel Langhorne (pen name for Mark Twain). *Innocents Abroad*. Daniel Morley McKeithen, ed. Norman: University of Oklahoma Press, 1958.

Crum, Bartley. *Behind the Silken Curtain* (A Personal Account of Anglo-American Diplomacy in Palestine and the Middle East). New York: Simon and Schuster, 1947.

Fink, Reuben. *America and Palestine* (The Attitude of Official America and of the American People Toward the Rebuilding of Palestine as a Free and Democratic Jewish Commonwealth). New York: Herald Square Press, 1945.

Fishman, Hertzel. *American Protestantism and a Jewish State*. Detroit: Wayne State University Press, 1973.

Friedrich, Carl J. *American Policy Toward Palestine*. Washington: Public Affairs Press, 1944.

Halperin, Samuel. *The Political World of American Zionism*. Detroit: Wayne State University Press, 1961.

Hoopes, Townsend. *The Devil and John Foster Dulles*. Boston: Atlantic-Little, Brown, 1973.

Hurewitz, J. C. *The Struggle for Palestine*. New York: Norton, 1950.

Institute for Palestine Studies, ed. *Christians, Zionism and Palestine*. Beirut, I.P.S., 1970.

Johnson, R. Park, Middle East Representative, United Presbyterian Church, 1950–1967. Personal interview.

Kautsky, Karl. *Foundations of Christianity, A Study in Christian Origins*. New York and London: Monthly Review Press, 1971. Originally published by International Publishers, Co., Inc., 1925.

King, Michael Christopher, staff of the World Council of Churches. *A Sketch of the Structure of Ecumenical Work with Palestine Refugees*. Typescript.

Leon, Abram. *The Jewish Question: A Marxist Interpretation*. New York: Pathfinder Press, 1970.

Lewis, Dean, Director, Advisory Council on Church and Society, United Presbyterian Church. Personal interview.

Manuel, Frank E. *The Realities of American-Palestine Relations*. Washington: Public Affairs Press, 1949.

The Middle East Council of Churches, Department on Service to Palestine Refugees, *Annual Report 1978*.

Musallam, Basim. "Power and Knowledge, a Review Essay of Edward Said's *Orientalism*" in MERIP REPORTS, No. 79, IX, 5, June 1979, pp. 19–26.

National Council of Churches. *An Affirmation of Hope for Peace in the Middle East*, adopted by the Executive Committee, December 13, 1974.

National Council of Churches. *In the Global Village*, Church World Service Annual Report 1978.

National Council of Churches. *On the Crisis in the Middle East, A Policy Statement Adopted by the General Board*, May 2, 1969.

National Council of Churches. *Resolution on Ambassador Young and the Middle East*, adopted by the Executive Committee, September 7, 1979.

Rubin, Jacob A. *Partners in State-Building: American Jewry & Israel*. New York: Diplomatic Press, 1969.

Said, Edward. *Orientalism*. New York: Pantheon, 1978.

Schechtman, Joseph B. *The United States and the Jewish State Movement: The Crucial Decade: 1939-1949*. New York: Herzl Press, 1966.

Sokolow, Nahum. *History of Zionism, 1600-1918*. Two volumes in one. New York: KTAV Publishing House, 1969.

Solomonow, Allan, ed. *Where We Stand: Official Statements of American Churches on the Middle East Conflict*. New York: The Middle East Consultation Group and the Middle East Peace Program, November 1977.

Stevens, Richard. *American Zionism and U.S. Foreign Policy, 1942-1947*. New York: Pageant Press, 1962.

Stone, Ronald, Professor at Pittsburgh Theological Seminary, biographer of Reinhold Niebuhr. Personal interview.

Stork, Joe. *Middle East Oil and the Energy Crisis*. New York: Monthly Review Press, 1975.

World Council of Churches. *Palestine Refugees—Aid With Justice, The Report of the Consultation on the Palestine Refugee Program*, Nicosia, Cyprus, September 29–October 4, 1969.

World Council of Churches. *Report From Beirut: A Report of a Conference on Arab Refugee Problems*, Beirut, Lebanon, May 4–8, 1951.

World Council of Churches. *Second Report from Beirut: A Report of a Conference on the Problem of Arab Refugees from Palestine*, Beirut, Lebanon, May 21–25, 1956.

5

Theology and Politics in the Middle East: Some Christian Reflections

Paul Jersild

Theological or religious beliefs have often been the source of political action, both good and bad. In a positive way, the religious convictions of a society undergird the social morality which in turn provides the necessary support of politics. Yet in a negative way, the mobilizing of religious sentiment for the purpose of effecting a political result has often had immoral and even dire consequences. Politics and religion come together at various levels of society's life and consciousness, but often the result is unfortunate because political leaders can and often do exploit religion for their own purposes. Or again, religious sentiment can result in a fanatical politics that can become demonic in its effects.

The current political struggle in the Near East provides an obvious and certainly unique example of the intermixture of theology and politics, posing difficult questions for Christians as well as Jews. For one thing, it raises the question of present-day Israel's meaning and destiny in light of the sacred scriptures shared by these two religions. Both religions believe that God is present and active in this world, and that the people of Israel have played a peculiar role in this divine activity. Does the Bible speak to the existence of Israel today? Should Christians treat the state of Israel as the fulfillment of Biblical promises? Is religion being misused in its application to the current struggle? This paper will address these questions particularly in view of the Old Testament (to use Christian terminology for the Jewish scriptures) references to "the land," and will draw some conclusions in regard to the Old Testament prophetic tradition in its relation to contemporary Israel.

ISRAEL AND THE LAND

In 1939, Zionist demonstrators who were protesting against the position taken by the British government carried signs which read "Not the British Mandate but the Bible is our title to this land." Whether or not one agrees with such a statement, it does reveal a common and sincere belief among most Jews and Zionists in particular that they stand in a continuous line with the Old Testament. A promise of a land which runs prominently throughout the Old Testament is regarded by Zionists as a promise to God's Chosen People in the 20th century which has now found its fulfillment.

The importance of the land to the Old Testament faith has always been recognized, but in recent years the subject has found renewed interest among Biblical scholars.[1] Walter Brueggemann claims that "Land is a central, if not *the central theme* of biblical faith," and a fruitful category for organizing Biblical theology.[2] Much of Israel's history is a struggle for the land, where the faithful are alternately sojourners, wanderers, and victims of exile, as well as settlers and keepers of the land. As one follows the Biblical story, the land which is at one time a promise becomes later a problem, with prosperity and power under the monarchy leading to exploitation from within and national defeat and slavery from without. The relation of Israel to the land is a story of both fulfillment of a people's hopes and dreams and judgment of a people's faithlessness to their covenantal relation to God who they believed had given them the land.

Clearly the land as both promise and problem is very much at the forefront of Israel's life today. It seems an inevitable dimension of its existence. The point often made today by Jewish authors is that the very identity of their people is dependent upon their relation to the land.

> To deny Israel's right to live its corporate life as a nation is to deny its right to exist. To invite the Jews to live as Jews and to be faithful to "Judaism" without fulfilling their existence in what had previously been defined as the "hypostatic union" of people and land is sheer hypocrisy . . . . the announced "politicide" of Israel implies, and is meant to imply, genocide.[3]

The Zionist of the nineteenth century, Moses Hess, maintained that "it is the land that we lack in order to exercise our religion," an assertion which unites the land with the religious self-consciousness of the Jew. The typical Israeli today is rather far removed from an active participation in the religious heritage of his people (symbolic of the secular spirit is the fact that synagogues are difficult to find in the *kibbutzim* of the land), yet the uniting of land and religion is a prominent feature of Israel's claim to the land. It is fair to say that even the least religious of the Israeli somehow regard Palestine as belonging to them on ultimately religious grounds—the land is theirs by divine right.

Among Christians this sentiment is ardently affirmed by many, including the eminent Roman Catholic philosopher, Jacques Maritain, who regards it as "divinely certain" that the Israeli have an incontestable right to Palestine. ". . . what God has given once is given forever." Any criticism of Zionism is seen by Maritain as a covert form of anti-Semitism. This raises a very tender issue, for there is considerable guilt among Christians today over the treatment of Jews by nations whose religious institutions have been shaped by the Christian tradition, culminating in the horrors of Nazi Germany. In an effort to avoid the charge of anti-Semitism, Christians are easily coerced into muting or totally suppressing any criticism they might think justified concerning Israel and the Zionist cause. The acceptance of the Jew is virtually made equivalent to the acceptance of Israel's politics in its claim to the land.

INTERPRETING THE BIBLICAL TEXTS

For the Christian who accepts the Bible as a book of faith which witnesses to God's deeds in history, the relation of Israel to the land of Palestine is a matter that must be taken seriously. This involves the interpretation of Biblical texts, asking their meaning for today after having determined to our satisfaction their meaning for the day in which they were written. Much Christian writing on this subject suffers from a lack of historical sense, in which the writer proceeds as though the text has a fairly obvious meaning directed to our own time. Any reference to the future made by the Biblical writer is regarded as a prediction, bearing a single meaning which we should be able to see if we take it according to its literal truth. It is more accurately the case that, even within the Bible itself, certain promises are reinterpreted and take on quite new dimensions of meaning as the Israelites are confronted by new and challenging historical circumstances. The texts dealing with the land provide a rich example of this truth.[4]

The promise of a land is an idea that occurs over thirty times in the first five books of the Old Testament (the Pentateuch). It is a promise from God in the first person, often accompanied by an oath in order to underscore the certainty of the promise. It is rather commonly agreed that this promise was a part of pre-Mosaic patriarchal religion, an important element in the hopes and dreams of a people living at the edge of a land already settled. But an interesting transformation takes place in the book of Genesis. What is at first a simple promise to the patriarchs of a land which shall be theirs is later reinterpreted so that the promise finds its fulfillment at a much later date, in the time of Joshua. In addition, the revision in the understanding of promise extends its scope to apply to all the people of Israel, not just to the patriarchs.

Another tradition that appears in this material is that expressed in Leviticus 25:23: "The land is mine; you are only sojourners." According to the tradition attributed to the Yahwist, the land belongs to the nations, while here, from a priestly perspective, the land belongs to God. This conviction gives rise to the sabbatical year and tithes and offerings. Or again, in the book of Deuteronomy, obedience to God's commandments is seen as the precondition to possessing the land. Since at the time of this writing the Israelites are already in possession of the land, the book of Deuteronomy introduces the notion of an eschatological future, a future of promise that awaits those who are faithful today. A further spiritualization of the promise is seen in various Psalms, where the cultic emphasis upon the theme "God is my portion" constitutes the hope and promise to which the religious Jew looks forward (cf. Psalm 142:5; 16:5 ff.).

The Old Testament prophets make their own distinctive contribution to the understanding of the promise and the land. There is considerable reinterpretation of the promise which emerges in a new vision of the future—seen dramatically in Jeremiah, chapters 30 to 33—in which a return to the land is associated with faithfulness to the covenant. For the Jews in exile, the promise of the land is a promise of return to the land of their ancestors: "You shall dwell in the land which I gave to your fathers; and you shall be my people and I will be your God" (Ezekiel 36:28). In each case, traditions from the past provide inspiration for a new vision of the future in which the original tradition is enlarged well beyond its earlier meaning.

In the Christian scriptures, the New Testament, we see a continuation of this process of reinterpretation. The letter to the

Hebrews transforms the Zion tradition into a heavenly city, a city not made by human hands but prepared by God. Rather than a homeland to which the faithful will return, "they desire a better country, that is, a heavenly one" (Heb. 11:16). The writer to the Ephesians refers to the "inheritance" promised to the saints as no longer the land but the promise of fulfillment to life that stretches into the future that God has prepared. Paul speaks of sonship and freedom as the blessings the heir receives from his father. Christians see here a spiritualizing and enlarging of the promise made possible by the death and resurrection of Jesus Christ, through whom the promise is universalized to encompass all people. His own legacy for the believer explodes the sense of place from a land to a family of God that would transcend every boundary we might impose upon it.

On the other hand, for Jews it is understandable that the tradition in which they stand quite naturally asks to be reinterpreted once again as it is applied to the current situation. What could be more natural, given the tradition of promise and the land, than the application of that promise to the ancient homeland of today? It is for the faithful in every generation to draw out the implications of the promise as they see it for themselves. When Theodore Herzl began the Zionist movement, the presence of the promise directed to the land literally begged for reinterpretation in that particular situation. It quite naturally continues to inspire Israeli hopes today in a far different situation, where Israel is now a sovereign nation but forced to defend its right to the land against hostile neighbors.

With this recognition of the continuing need to reinterpret the promise, we must also recognize the misuse of that promise today in the interpretations made by many Christians as well as Jews. That misuse is seen in the attempt to use passages from the Old Testament as "proof texts" to demonstrate Israel's *right* to the land in the twentieth century. This approach reveals a misunderstanding of the nature of these passages. The history of the tradition of "land and promise" indicates that the promises made in various times and places are affirmations or a witness concerning the goodness of God rather than proofs or predictions which can be directly related to historical situations quite different from the situation which gave rise to them. As Hals observes:

> None of (these reinterpretations) attempts to convince others who do not share their presuppositions by presenting an argument which will demonstrate the inescapable logical force of their conclusions. Rather than endeavoring to prove, they affirm. Said another way, what

these reinterpretations do is to look back, affirming that their present situation constitutes a fulfillment of previous promises, and to look ahead, affirming that the future under God's control will bring no ultimate frustration of those promises. To label such affirmations "proof from prophecy" is to use terminology of an inappropriate sort. Or to attempt today to prove to some disinterested court a legal claim or a historical right of Jews to possess this land on the basis of such passages seems to involve an illegitimate use of them, to say nothing of any efforts to determine boundaries on such a basis.[5]

To the secular world, the uniting of theology and politics in this day and age constitutes at least a bizarre oddity if not a dangerous absurdity. Thus the summoning of an ancient sacred scripture to validate a modern nation-state is dismissed out of hand. For Christians it is not quite so simple. The scriptures and witness of the church convince them of God's involvement in a particular history and a particular place. The critical task is to rightly interpret the sacred history in its implications for politics and geography today. I have argued that a proper understanding of the texts will avoid their literalistic or legalistic application to today's world. It is not possible to prescribe a political or military solution from the scriptures for international problems today, whether in the Near East or anywhere else.

From the Christian point of view, of course, there is the additional and quite crucial factor of Jesus Christ and his impact on the Old Testament tradition. As a Christian I see the meaning of Judaism today in terms of a testimony of a particular people to the goodness of God, whose will was embodied and revealed in one of their own in such a decisive way that a new order and a new age was initiated in our history. The geographical dimension of the sacred history was transformed by Jesus Christ into a cosmic message of divine grace. This development, as far as I can see, leaves the Christian with no theological directive concerning the present state of Israel. Neither from the Old Testament nor the New Testament can the Christian effectively argue for a geographical destiny for the twentieth century Jew. There may of course be other grounds on which one might want to make a case for the state of Israel, but not on theological or Biblical grounds.

ISRAEL, THE LAND, AND THE PROPHETIC TRADITION

There is another part of the Old Testament tradition that bears consideration in this discussion. It is the prophetic tradition in its proclamation of judgment on the people of Israel. For the non-Jew living in the twentieth century, this part of the Old Testament tradition is undoubtedly the most viable as a message that speaks to today's world.It is of interest to us here because of its implications for the notion that Israel has a divine claim upon the land of its fathers.

Norman Gottwald observes that the claims for nationhood by the Jews are not unambiguously supported by the prophetic tradition. The prophets regarded the exile of the sixth century B.C. as a necessary discipline, with the survival of Israel understood in a "religio-cultural sense."[6] The unknown prophet called Deutero-Isaiah recognized a religious triumph in Israel's history while the Jews were subject to the Persian empire. "It remained an open question whether Israel was to have political identity, and if so, whether it would be imperialistic."[7]

The particular message of the prophets is that land and covenant cannot be separated—with inheritance there must also be fidelity to Yahweh. The religious and moral judgment that is so often and so eloquently delivered by Isaiah, Amos, Micah, Hosea, and Jeremiah among others is always a reminder to the people of Israel that more is expected of them than of other nations. They are reminded that the land is a gift, not their own possession. Their loss of the land is seen as a work of divine retribution, for God uses the nations to work his judgment.

We must be careful here that we do not make the same mistake that we have accused others of making in the use of scripture. We cannot use the prophets as a basis for understanding the defeats of Israel today as a divine judgment, just as we would not want to understand Israel's victories as expressions of divine approbation. This direct and simplistic use of scripture is not acceptable in the realm of judgment any more than in the realm of promise—yet there is something about the prophetic message together with the peculiar faith of the Jews that raises an issue for Israeli self-understanding at the present time.

Markus Barth states the issue well:

> . . . we must remind the Israelis (a) that the Bible does not speak of an ownership of soil and land but of a stewardship of God's property (e.g., Lev. 25:23); (b) that in the land which God has promised the stranger born in the land shall stand under the same law as the Jew (Exod. 12:49; Lev. 24:22; Num. 9:14; 15:15-16) and (c) that righteousness and mercy are not possible tasks *after* the battle for survival but are the prerequisites for life itself (Deut. 30:16; Lev. 18:5).[8]

If the use of sacred scripture to justify national policies and objectives is not to be idolatrous and self-serving, then those who interpret those scriptures must be willing to listen to the divine command as well as the promise. It is quite easy to equate the Gush Emunim with the ancient patriarch to whom a land is promised, but the question is whether there is any integrity left to the tradition when applied in this way.

Not only the prophetic message, but also the Jewish liturgies and the Talmud bring a challenge to Israeli self-understanding. These sources clearly give priority to people over the land, and to the land over statehood.[9] Most references to the land are expressed without reference to David, the symbol of national sovereignty. From a Christian viewpoint, this distinction is certainly valid today. Support for the Jewish people cannot be understood as automatic or unqualified support for the right of the state of Israel to exist. That right would certainly, among other things, call for Israel to grant equal rights to *all* the inhabitants of their land instead of placing non-Jews under the onus of second-class citizenship.

One can of course fault other nations for being no better than Israel, but that is beside the point here. The religious tradition to which Israelis appeal calls on them to be "proexistent," a sign among the nations which reflects the higher calling of God. If they claim a sense of "chosenness," of being a people of divine destiny, then their religious tradition would also beckon them to a peculiar national purpose. That purpose would be demonstrated by subjecting their nationalistic aspirations to a probing self-criticism in the spirit of their prophetic tradition.

It is a sobering fact that the establishment of modern-day Israel as a sovereign nation could not have occurred without the immense moral support gained among Western nations for a people who had been subjected to unbelievable torture and grief. The very pathos of the Jews provided the necessary support among the nations. It is a painful ambiguity that now this people whose burden of suffering brought such international support are themselves disposing of other peoples' lives and destiny. In some sense, of course, all nations find themselves in this position, but Christians should not be regarded as presumptuous if they ask whether the historic tradition to which the Israeli appeal does not challenge their use of power. There is a deep sense of tragedy in the picture of the twentieth century Israel seeking to maintain its heritage and identity by means of an imperialist state.

POLITICAL REALITIES FOR ISRAEL

There is a small minority of Israelis who take issue with their nation's use of military power and who advocate a more humane foreign policy. In some instances their concerns are motivated by religious conviction, but there are also those who argue a better way on pragmatic grounds:

> An Israeli general, who was given early retirement, told me that security could not all be guaranteed by military means. It could rest only on the confidence of the Palestinians in the Jews and on good relationships between both. . . . One day, a stronger minority in Israel than only five percent will think as he does. [10]

A similar viewpoint is expressed by a professor at Hebrew University:

> "Israel may be able to win and win and go on winning 'til its last breath, win itself to death. . . . After every victory, we face more difficult, more complicated problems. . . . The abyss of mutual hatred will deepen and the desires for vengeance will mount."[11]

Quite apart from the Biblical heritage, there are good reasons for placing the principal responsibility for peace in the Middle East on Israel. As one nation whose enemies are disparate states with competing interests, Israel has greater potential for flexibility and taking the initiative in improving Arab-Israeli relationships. More than any one nation, Israel is in a position to exploit the possibilities of increasing trust between Arabs and the Israelis.

The challenge to Israel posed by Near East realities is to move beyond the Zionist mentality. This challenge has been eloquently expressed, among others, by Uri Avnery:

> Joining a great Semitic confederacy would mean, for Israel, putting an end to the Zionist chapter in its history and starting a new one—the chapter of Israel as a state integrated in its Region, playing a part in the Region's struggle for progress and unity.[12]

A noble vision has been shared by a few on both sides over the last few decades, marked by reconciliation and unity. The Jewish philosopher Martin Burber, at the XII Zionist Congress in 1921, proposed a program in which both Jews and Palestinians would counteract the methods of capitalism and imperialism by mutually developing Palestine on the basis of common labor on common ground. In 1963 Buber protested bitterly that this possibility had been thwarted by power politics and colonialism. A new direction beyond Zionism is urgently needed, not alone on the grounds of the religious and moral insights of the prophets, but because the political and military realities demand of Israel a new policy of reconciliation with her neighbors if she is going to survive.

That minority in Israel today who reflect the prophetic faith and who point most persuasively to a better future in Arab-Israeli relationships are those who renounce the military "solution" in behalf of an aggressive campaign for reconciliation and understanding. As one reflects on the message of Israel's tradition for the state of Israel today, it can be expressed quite well in the thesis at which Walter Brueggemann arrives in his engaging work on Israel and the land. He concludes that throughout Israel's history the *grasp* for land paradoxically brings the *loss* of land,[13] and Israel is challenged today as never before to learn that hard lesson. Those who have learned it are those who now actively engage in the struggle for peace through reconciliation. In the long run, there is no other way.

NOTES

1. Two recent works on the subject are Walter Brueggemann, *The Land* (Philadelphia: Fortress Press, 1977) and W. D. Davies, *The Gospel and the Land* (Berkeley: U. of California Press, 1974).
2. Cf. Brueggemann, pp. 3ff.
3. Zwi Werblowsky, "The People and the Land," *Speaking of God Today: Jews and Lutherans in Conservation.* Ed. Paul D. Opsahl and Marc H. Tanenbaum (Philadelphia: Fortress, 1974), p. 80.
4. For an excellent overview of Christian Old Testament scholarship on the subject of promise and the land, see Gerhard von Rad, "The Promised Land and Yahweh's Land in the Hexateuch," in his *The Problem of the Hexateuch and Other Essays* (Edinburgh, London: Oliver & Boyd, 1966), pp. 79-93. Ronald M. Hals discusses this essay and provides some reflective conclusions in his article, "The Promise and the Land," in Opsahl and Tanenbaum, pp. 57-72. The discussion of the next few paragraphs is based on Hals' article.
5. Hals, pp. 68-69.
6. Norman K. Gottwald, *All the Kingdoms of the Earth* (N.Y.: Harper & Row, 1964), p. 391.

7. *Ibid.*

8. Markus Barth, *Jesus the Jew* (Atlanta: John Knox Press, 1978), p. 93.

9. Barth, pp. 94–95.

10. Barth, p. 61.

11. Quoted in American Friends Service Committee, *Search for Peace in the Middle East*, rev. ed. (Greenwich, Conn.: Fawcett, 1970), p. 78.

12. Uri Avnery, *Israel Without Zionists* (N.Y.: Macmillan, 1968), p. 210.

13. "The central learning about the Land motif which has come out of this study is that grasping for home leads for homelessness and risking homelessness yields the gift of home" (p. 189). ???

6

Religion and U.S. Foreign Policy Towards the Middle East: A Catholic Perspective

Rev. Joseph L. Ryan, S. J.

The focus of this paper is the Roman Catholic Church especially in the United States and its relation to United States foreign policy towards the Middle East. That relation is most clearly expressed by official documents, and it is these which I shall examine. Sources not considered here are writings of U.S. Catholic groups or individuals (such as in newspapers or publications of organizations), or actions of Catholic groups and individuals. (See Esther Yolles Teldblum, *American Catholic Press and the Jewish State 1917-1959*, N.Y., KTAV 1977).

What documents have the U.S. bishops issued on the Middle East? Three are not important for our purposes, two of which concerned the internationalization of Jerusalem (November 17, 1949 and November 20, 1950), and the third entitled "Tensions and Conflict in the Middle East" (September 1, 1969), was a general overview of the Middle East. I shall dwell on the other seven; they are as follows:

1) November 13, 1973 statement "Towards Peace in the Middle East," and a background statement "The Structure of the Question" by Rev. J. Bryan Hehir, Associate Director, Division of International Justice and Peace.

2) September 3, 1975 statement by Archbishop Joseph L. Bernadin, President of the U.S. Catholic Conference, opposing attempts to suspend or drive Israel out of the United Nations and repeating the central elements of the 1973 statement.

3) November 11, 1975 statement by Archbishop Bernadin deploring the United Nations resolution equating Zionism with racism.

4) January 23, 1976 statement by Archbishop Bernadin on Lebanon and the Middle East.

5) August 15, 1978 statement by Archbishop John R. Quinn, President of the National Conference of U.S. Catholic Bishops, on "The Crisis in Lebanon."

6) October 31, 1978 statement of Archbishop Quinn on Lebanon.

7) November 16, 1978 statement of the National Conference of U.S. Bishops on "The Pursuit of Peace with Justice," reiterating the 1973 statement and also discussing Lebanon, Camp David, and Beyond Camp David.

What do these statements say? One of them rejects the U.N. resolution on Zionism as racism. Another opposes attempts at the suspension or expulsion of Israel from the U.N. Both of these statements are supportive of the U.N. Four of the statements, January 1976, August, October, and November 1978, are concerned with Lebanon. What do they say? Without going into great detail and without trying to explain the different settings and the nuances of each statement, one can say that the bishops see the need for understanding the complexity of the Middle East (its internal religious, economic, political aspects, and its special pluralism) and the relation of the Lebanese situation to conditions in the area (regional peace is needed for Lebanon but is not sufficient). The bishops express a special concern for Christian communities in Lebanon. They call for help from the United States, from the international community, and from the United Nations. They call for the preservation of the cease-fire, the rebuilding of the Lebanese army, the establishment of a new Lebanese constitution, and the preservation of the sovereignty and the neutrality of Lebanon.

Three of the statements (1973, 1976, November 1978) treat the Arab-Israeli conflict. There is continuing emphasis on several central elements. In the form given in November 1978, they are as follows:

1) The rights of Israel: to existence as a sovereign state within secure and recognized boundaries;

2) The rights of the Palestinian Arabs: to participate in negotiations affecting their destiny, and to a homeland of their own;

3) Compensation: just compensation should be provided for all parties concerned, of whatever national origin, deprived of home and property by the three decades of conflict;

4) The status of Jerusalem: recognition of its unique religious significance which should be preserved through an international

guarantee of access to the holy places, and through the preservation of a religiously pluralist citizenry;

5) U.N. Resolution 242: its continuing utility as a basis for a just settlement in the region.

The last (1978) statement speaks of the Camp David accords and beyond. The Camp David accords "have an intrinsic value which ought to be praised and supported and they have limitations which need to be acknowledged and amended." Among the limitations two are specified: the status of Jerusalem and the fate of the Palestinians. Several parties must have roles: the international community, especially "its principal diplomatic actors," the United Nations, the regional parties, and the religious communities with roots in the Middle East.

Who are addressed by these statements? The statements expressly or indirectly appeal to a variety of parties:

—to men and women of good will (1973) and faith (October 1978); to the U.S. public (October 1978), public opinion (August 1978);

—to American Catholics (1973, 1976, August 1978, October 1978), to "the Christian Church" (1976), to (U.S.) religious communities with roots in the Middle East (October 1978);

—to local churches in the Middle East (October 1978), to the inhabitants of the Holy Land (October 1978);

—to all the people of Lebanon (October 1978, August 1978), to the Lebanese religious leaders (October 1978), and to the Catholic bishops of Lebanon (August 1978);

—to Palestinians to accept Israel's right to exist (1976);

—to the U.N. especially the Secretary General (October 1978), and to the international community (1976, October 1978);

—to President Carter (October 1978), to U.S. policy makers (August 1978), to the U.S. "to set an example of disinterested and constructive diplomacy in the Middle East; . . . to take explicitly the position that the Palestinians be included as partners in future negotiations . . . " (1976), to the U.S. not to implement the U.N. resolution on Zionism as racism and not to diminish U.S. support of the U.N. (1975);

—to the U.S. and the USSR for restraint (1973).

The variety of parties addressed is interesting, in fact, significant. What is behind it? In the November 1978 statement, the bishops state that they wish to bring the Middle East problem before the Catholic community in the United States, "so that this universal challenge to conscience may be in their thoughts and prayers." The statement continues:

We seek also to make a constructive contribution to the public debate in a nation whose impact on the Middle East is recognized throughout the world. We realize that the specific technical questions at the heart of the Middle East conflict must be resolved in the diplomatic arena, but it is our conviction that on an issue at once so politically and emotionally significant, public opinion in a society shapes the atmosphere for political choices. In accordance with this conviction we offer the following:

This emphasis is not new. In the 1973 statement the bishops explain that they spoke

as pastors concerned for the parties immediately involved, seeking to offer guidance to American Catholics on the issue, and later to do what we can, even from this distance, to contribute to a just, peaceful and lasting resolution of this painful tragedy.

At the end of their statement they state:

In proposing these reflections we seek to fulfill our ministry of justice and peace. We ask men and women of good will to consider them in the spirit in which they are offered, as a contribution to reconciliation in the Middle East and peace in the world.

They conclude by asking blessings "on our efforts and those peoples and governments who labor as peacemakers."

Having considered the statements of United States Catholic bishops, we can next reflect on their action.

1) At the highest level, they have spoken out repeatedly (7 times) and explicitly on the two central Middle East questions, the Arab-Israeli conflict and Lebanon. Two of the statements were issued in the name of all the bishops, the other five were issued in the name of the president of the bishops' conference.

2) The bishops take such action explicitly for two reasons: a) officially as U.S. Catholic bishops to give guidance to Catholics, and b) to contribute to the public debate.

A comment on this point is provided by remarks by Rev. J. Bryan Hehir, Associate Director of the U.S. Catholic Conference Division of Justice and Peace. Speaking on April 30, 1976 on a panel discussing U.S. churches and the Middle East, Fr. Hehir said that churches related to the Middle East in two ways, first, through ecclesiastical organizations, and secondly by individuals in "the primacy of the political." The Christian churches and the members belonging to them can enter into the policy debate. They cannot solve the Middle East problem nor even set the agenda, but as institutions and as individual citizens they can be actors by participating in the policy debate and by contributing ideas. The churches are not only major structures in the United States, they are major media as well. Explaining this point further on another occasion (in *Network Quarterly*, Vol. IV, No. 3, Summer 1976) Fr. Hehir stated that religious organizations were neither political parties nor research institutions. What they are uniquely equipped to do, however, is to form a constituency of conscience on lay foreign policy issues. By a constituency of conscience he means "a body of citizenry in the midst of the larger society which has a specific angle of vision on foreign policy questions involving significant moral content." In this process, people are not being told how to vote but are being helped to think and decide. The religious institutions take specific policy positions and then go to their constituencies to garner support. The office or group issuing the statement does not claim to speak for all Catholics but for institutional Catholicism. Having done so, the group goes to the Catholic community to form a concensus on the issue.

Why does the Catholic Church become involved politically? Fr. Hehir, speaking to a legislative seminar organized by Network (a group involved in advocacy and representing U.S. Catholic sisters), answered that question at great length (*Network Quarterly*, Vol. II, No. 3, Summer 1974). He defined "ministry of justice" thus: to apply the Gospel command of love through the virtue of social justice to complex human relationships." This ministry of justice, he said, which has been developing since the 1891 encyclical *Rerum Novarum*, has two characteristics: it has moved from the periphery of the Church's life towards its heart, and it has moved from being the work of specialists to being now regarded as a basic Christian responsibility. The process, Fr. Hehir said, involves three stages: the development of ideas, or principles; the creation of organizations to implement these ideas and principles; and institutional changes incorporating them. Furthermore, Fr. Hehir compared the preceding fifteen years of papal encyclical tradition with the earlier period (1871-1931). He found important characteristics. First, the unit of analysis has moved from the national community to the international. Secondly, there is a movement in the encyclicals from economics to politics. Thirdly, he finds an explicit assertion in papal social teaching of the importance of local or national churches in implementing a strategy of social justice.

What this record indicates is that the ministry of justice in the Roman Catholic church in the U.S. has great potential strength, is open, and, in the future, is likely to be increasingly active. These conclusions obviously should be of great interest to anyone concerned about possible changes in U.S. policy regarding the Middle East. These conclusions suggest the following four questions:

1. HOW DOES INSTITUTIONAL CATHOLICISM IN THE UNITED STATES COME TO ITS POLICY DECISIONS?

The process is described at length by Fr. Hehir (in *Network Quarterly*, Vol. IV, No. 3, Summer 1976, "Religious Organizations and International Affairs"; and in "Ethics and Foreign Policy: Creating a Constituency," an address given June 26, 1978). He contrasts the classical and the modernist views. The classicists' view took the nation-state as the unit of action of international affairs; the relationships of the nation-state involved "high politics," that is, political influence and military power (as against "low politics," that is, economics and other issues). But times have changed. Today the role of the nation-state is eroded but not eviscerated; military power is devalued but it remains in force in interstate relations; state boundaries are more porous, domestic economics are more vulnerable to outside forces. Over against the classicists, who stress the political-strategic agenda, the modernists speak the language of interdependence. Besides strategic power there is economic power (e.g. of the Organization of Petroleum Exporting Countries) and even moral power (e.g. the claims of the hungry become a force calling for change). While the state remains the unique agent in global politics, transnational actors and transnational problems make the idea of the self-sufficient insulated nation-state outmoded. Fr. Hehir believes that today religious communities must take both dimensions, the political-strategic and the political-economic, of the political process, must probe the specifics of each dimension, and must seek to relate the two parts of policy. The dominant political-strategic question is the arms race, but religious communities have shown little sustained interest (except regarding Vietnam) in the political strategic questions. This lack of interest suggests indifference to one of the central moral and political issues of the age. The dominant political-economic issue concerns the New International Economic Order. Here religious communities have shown interest.
    Fr. Hehir then goes on to examine the Middle East conflict as an

example of a problem involving both political-strategic issues and political-economic ones. The political-strategic aspect is clear: the Middle East conflict involves both the regional powers and also the superpowers. But the political-economic aspects are even clearer: in the October, 1973 war the oil weapon struck at the West and since then the OPEC group has been the pivotal group within the coalition of "77" working for a new international economic order. The peace and justice dimensions of the Middle East are stark and interconnected. Peace is threatened because any outbreak may escalate into a nuclear-superpower conflict. Justice is involved because the regional actors describe their claims in terms of justice. The United States must decide how much regional "stability" it will tolerate to preserve the peace, especially when one of the regional actors believes that its justice claim can be obtained only through force. Thus peace may be threatened either way. Fr. Hehir then goes on to examine the conflicting justice claims of Israel, the Palestinians, and the Arab states. He considers three aspects: sovereignty, security, and territory. Israelis stress territory and security, Palestinians territory and sovereignty, the Arab states a combination of their sovereignty and Palestinian territory. Faced with these three positions, what should the United States do? Fr. Hehir would distinguish between procedure and substance. Procedurally he would separate minimal from maximal positions. If no actor will realize his maximal demands (short of overwhelming his opponents), a state will fight if refused its minimal claims. How then to define the minimal claims and satisfy them all? Substantively, United States policy, Fr. Hehir states, might be as follows:

(a) Israel's *minimum* security position must be met, including *de facto* and *de jure* recognition by the Palestinians and the Arab states.

(b) The security solution must satisfy the minimum Palestinian claim for territory.

(c) The Palestinian claim for sovereignty cannot be foreclosed, although provision for meeting it can be left to negotiations.

(d) The second principle above requires implementation of United Nations Resolution 242 regarding withdrawal. The first principle requires that the Arab states and the Palestinians meet the other requirements of 242.

(e) The U.N. with superpower sponsorship should militarily watch the borders with peacekeeping forces and diplomatically monitor the settlement. Such an agreement would have to be "sold" to the parties. More than that, it should have to be sold to the American people.

2. WHAT PERSONS ARE INVOLVED IN THE PROCESS?

The statements we have reported were issued by the U.S. Catholic bishops and by their president. The bishops' office which has responsibility for these matters is the Office of International Justice and Peace. Its associate director is Rev. J. Bryan Hehir, a priest of the Boston archdiocese. He obtained his Ph.D. degree at Harvard and teaches at St. John's Seminary in Boston.

Are there other institutions within the Catholic church which influence the organizational structure in making foreign policy statements? There has been one unique and extraordinary instance. On October 20-23, 1976 a conference called "Call to Action" was convened in Detroit. It was the culmination of a two-year bicentennial celebration of the American Catholic Church. The 1200 delegates who included bishops, priests, religious and lay persons, constituted the first national assembly of the American Catholic community. Each diocese had been invited to hold parish discussions; the bishops had sponsored seven national hearings on issues. (See *Agenda for Justice, Basic Documents of the U.S. Church's Social Policy 1978-1983*, published by Quixote Center, Mt. Ranier, MD 20122). At Detroit a series of recommendations was made and submitted to the U.S. bishops. The bishops did not give an unqualified assent to them but accepted them in large part. Further, they assigned each recommendation to an appropriate bishops' committee for response and/or implementation. They also set up a special committee to draw up a five-year plan of social outreach and to report publicly each November on how the "Call to Action" recommendations are being implemented. The recommendations covered the following topics: Church, Nationhood, Family, Personhood, Neighborhood, Humankind, Ethnicity and Race, Work, and Multiple Topics. The topic Humankind included three topics: Education for Global Justice with eleven recommendations, Defense of Human Rights with thirteen, and Disarmament and Peace with eleven. No recommendation was concerned with the Middle East except for a single reference to Lebanon.

3. WHAT OUTSIDE INFLUENCES IMPINGE
ON THE PERSONS AND PROCESS?

In the background statement, "The Structure of the Question," accompanying the bishops' 1973 statement, Fr. Hehir stated that regarding the Middle East the policy issue concerns not only foreign affairs but also religion and religious ties. He identified three ties: first, the tie to Christians in the Middle East "as members of the household of faith"; second, ties with the Jewish community "to whom we are committed not only in fellowship but religiously linked as Vatican II declares"; the tie to Vatican policy. Fr. Hehir argued that the Church should first address the foreign policy issues on their own merits, and in the light of decisions thus made the Church should look to the religious links it has. This reverses the more usual order. "Too often statements from religious bodies ignore or do not deal specifically with these larger issues. The concern for the . . . ecumenical problem overshadows other elements for which we are also responsible."

The importance of this point of view cannot be overstressed. It is particularly pertinent in the light of the very great pressure by some Jewish groups on all segments of American society to win support for Israel, especially after the 1967 war. Fr. Hehir's statement is all the more significant given his role in the office of International Peace and Justice. In the Vatican, likewise, a sharp distinction has been made between interfaith affairs and affairs of the state. For example, persons engaged in the Jewish-Catholic dialogue are not competent to speak on matters touching Vatican foreign relations.

4. WHAT ARE FUTURE PROSPECTS?

I am examining this question from the point of view of those concerned with justice for the Palestinians. First of all, while the value of the bishops' statements may be debated, anyone who considers them significant should also be aware from the analysis given in this paper of the comprehensive foreign policy point of view given by Fr. Hehir. That is, primacy is given not to ecumenical considerations but to the issues themselves in their overall framework. Hence, any approach that is analytical has the best chance of being persuasive. Secondly, the aspect of "the ministry of justice" is being given greater stress. The Catholic Church increasingly feels the necessity of addressing issues involving justice. For example, in his 1973 background paper Fr. Hehir argues for considering the importance of including Palestinians. He writes:

The Palestinians, because of their status, is the party which has the least chance of being counted as an independent element in any Middle East settlement. Yet, it could be argued that no other party to the conflict has suffered more over the past 25 years. It is both politically sound and morally necessary that the Palestinians be accepted as an independent participant in any negotiations on the

Middle East problem. They should not be simply a dependent variable in the equation, a party whose future is totally determined by other actors. I think the Church should stand for this form of independent presence for the Palestinians because here as in other areas of international life the weakest party becomes the forgotten party. Part of the Church's role in international affairs is to raise the forgotten factors to the level of conscious consideration, politically and ethically.

7

Christian Zionism in America: The Religious Factor in American Middle East Policy

Hassan S. Haddad

INTRODUCTION

Arab observers of American Middle East policy and of American public opinion on the Arab-Israeli conflict have always wondered about the depth of American pro-Israel sentiment. The expressed American "moral commitment" to Israel is often blamed on the great influence of the Jews on American public opinion, and on Zionist pressure on government officials. Among the institutions held responsible for this great influence are the Zionist organizations, the Israel Lobby in Washington, the printed and electronic media which are dominated by Jewish business. An indefinite political force called the Jewish vote, especially in key states such as New York and California, is often held responsible for pro-Israel attitudes of senators, governors, representatives, and the President of the United States.

But there is something missing in this explanation of the unusual relationship between America and Israel. The influence of the Israel Lobby and the Jewish vote, also the assessment of Jewish influence over the media, are sometimes overrated. But even if they are not, they cannot satisfactorily explain the depth and breadth of the American commitment to Israel on both the official and the popular levels, nor do they account for the readiness with which pro-Israel decisions are made. For even in areas where the Jewish vote is negligible or nonexistent, the pro-Israel bias is found. Politicians from such areas vote pro-Israel, and speak pro-Israel, even when, to outside observers, it appears that they do not have to. The platforms of both the democratic and the republican parties never fail to deal with issues vital to Israel, while ignoring other countries of interest to other American ethnic groups.

President Somoza of Nicaragua, in a national television appearance in April 1979, was pleading his case with the American public. He volunteered to assert that his regime always stood by Israel and voted pro-Israel at the United Nations. There was nothing in the questions of the interviewers to require such a statement. He made it because he knew it was popular with the American public. The unusual personal diplomacy of Secretary Kissinger and of President Carter in Middle East negotiations, unprecedented in the annals of American foreign policy, indicates that Israel truly has a special status in America's heart, not simply in its foreign policy.

The volume and quality of the coverage of Israeli stories and other Israel-oriented material in the American media could not be explained solely by influence from the top. American politicians, like the American media, operate on the principle of appealing to the established views of their constituents. They manipulate their public by doing and saying, or appearing to do and say, what the public wants. The gospel of the business community, "the customer is always right," applies also to the government and the media.

Extensive campaigns to "educate" the public in certain important matters, such as the energy crisis, the SALT (Strategic Arms Limitations Treaty) agreements, the recognition of China, and the Panama Canal treaties, indicate a willingness on the part of the administration to attempt to change public opinion on these matters. But American policy towards Israel during the past thirty years changed steadily only in one direction: more support, more aid, more commitment. When President Carter attempted to sell the public the idea of a national home for the Palestinians and the inclusion of the Soviet Union in the negotiation process, he was rebuffed, not only by Zionists and pro-Zionist activists, but apparently by the general public. In this case, the blending of pro-Israel public sentiment with anti-Soviet mania created a strong current of public opinion against the President. He had to change his course.

In other words, the pro-Israel anti-Arab sentiment of the American public is an important factor in the making of public policy vis-a-vis the Arab-Israeli conflict. It is the hypothesis of this study that this public sentiment is primarily the product of a strong and deep religious conviction which is not based on reasoned considerations of economic and political matters, or on knowledge of international politics.

This study will deal with the cultural, religious, and theological principles that led to such bias. We shall consider this bias on many levels: the common man, the clergy, and the theologians dealing with a religious-mystical issue. This will be limited to American Protestants, the "liberal" and the "conservative" wings. Protestant denominations in America represent a substantial majority with a substantial influence. (Catholics and Jews are excluded only because of space. They deserve a separate study.)

The religious roots of this American pro-Israel attitude produces a subliminal as well as a conscious influence on the views of the churches, the religious groups, the religious media, and the church goers. It is apparent that this attitude, although pro-Israel, is not always, or necessarily, pro-Jewish—a fact which does not at all inhibit the Zionist organizations in America and Israel from using and exploiting it to the fullest extent.

The study will also deal with the active influence of this current of pro-Zionist, pro-Israel attitude, by examining the strength of the churches and church organizations. The immense volume of religious literature that deals totally or partially with Israel and the Jews from a "Christian" or "Christian Zionist" point of view indicates the existence of very strong and extensive influence. The increase in importance and in membership of evangelical denominations, and the growth of the movement of Jews for Christ, is another proof of the widespread network of Christian Zionism in America. The limited progress, felt especially after 1973, in producing a more "evenhanded" attitude among liberal intellectuals is very small in extent compared to that of the religious pro-Israel orientation among the evangelical groups.

CHRISTIAN ZIONISM IN AMERICA

The cornerstone of Christian support of Israel is the equation of modern political Israel with the Biblical Israel. Since this is one of the basic tenets of Zionism, therefore this Biblically oriented Christian support of Israel is, in fact, Christian Zionism.

Christian Zionism is not only found among fundamentalist Protestants. Some of the most active spokesmen of this movement are found among Presbyterians, Lutherans, Episcopalians, and Catholics. Their activities on behalf of the Jewish State consist of support on the pulpit, in Sunday School teaching, articles in religious journals, pamphlets and handouts, and expensive advertising in national newspapers. Religious radio and television programs, which are growing in number and in audience, are filled with implied and explicit support of the State of Israel, and with calls for Christians to "understand and love the Jews and the State of Israel." There is an abundance of programs for tourism and study in Israel. The gamut of this pro-Israel propaganda goes from the crude, unqualified support of Zionism and the Jewish State and hatred for the Arabs (often in the company of communists) to the sophisticated theological justification of the "return of the exiles to the Promised Land in accordance with the eschatology of the scriptures."

Often "liberal" protestant and catholic views contain some measure of Christian temperance and concern for fellow man in expressing sympathy for the plight of the Palestinian refugees. This concern is strong enough to lead to a denunciation of the "Palestinians' fellow Arabs for not giving refuge to their brethren," and, at times, a slap on Israel's wrist for some of its "harsh measures" towards "Palestinian terrorists." This, however, does not destroy the image of Israel as a fulfillment of God's plan for history, or of its right to exist.

THEOLOGICAL BASIS OF CHRISTIAN ZIONISM

A quick survey of examples of theological and Biblical statements by Christian Zionists, extending from sophisticated theology to obsessive prophecy, will suffice to show the great permeability of this movement in the Christian Church in America.

The most moderate theological views on Israel, its place in the "scheme of things" and the duty of Christians in formulating United States policy in the Middle East, finds expression in a passage from the book *Christian Faith and Public Policy* by the Lutheran theologian Richard John Neuhaus.[1]

> The U.S. has a signal responsibility to Israel. The churches may and should protest specific policies of Israel, deplore the injustices by which the State of Israel came into being, and plead the plight of Palestinians and others who have been treated with great injustice by Israelis and Arabs alike.

The author (who had consulted a number of Lutheran theologians on the contents of his book) discharges, in this carefully worded sentence, his moral responsibility as a Christian to the oppressed Palestinians. Having done so he goes into the theological heart of the matter:

> Yet the steadiness and dependability of U.S. commitment to Israel's survival as a state must never be permitted to be thrown into question. We can hope that commitment will increasingly be shared by other powers, but if necessary the United States must stand alone with Israel.

This political statement, expressed with such finality, must have a religious-theological basis. The formulation of a Christian theology of Zionism has to rest on a mystery to be able to dismiss the "injustices" as temporary and temporal, and, as such, cannot interfere in a great divine scheme. The author goes on:

> This thinking about Israel is singularly affected by the relationship between living Judaism and the Church, a relationship which remains a great *mystery* and is marked by a much tortured history. In this relationship God has exercised judgment beginning with the household of faith. (Emphasis added.)

The support of Israel, therefore, should transcend the question of human rights, of injustice, of common political, social and economic considerations. The *mystical* foundation of Christian Zionism having been set, the author moves to the question of Christian guilt, another mainstay of Zionist philosophy.

> Lutheran Christians have particular reason to be aware of that judgment in view of the European Holocaust.

The guilt feeling expressed here has a double edge. Lutherans being Christians and, mostly, of German origin, must bear a double load of guilt-feeling for the "European Holocaust."

All this theologizing about Israel is, of course, predicated on identifying Israel with Judaism and the Jews all over the world, and of the continuity of the concept of Israel and of the Jewish people over thousands of years. The author is unequivocal about this point:

> It is necessary to distinguish, but it is not possible to separate, Israel from Judaism. Many people, both Christians and Jews, believe that upon the survival of the State of Israel may well depend the survival of living Judaism. Some Christians may strongly disagree with that evaluation, but we cannot gamble with the prospect of its turning out to be accurate.

Neuman's concern about the survival of Israel and of living Judaism comes from a common Christian belief in the centrality of the Jews, as God's Chosen People, to the fulfillment of God's plan for human history. The seeds of prophetic and millenarian convictions of conservative Protestants are found in this "liberal" statement by a Lutheran theologian. He has "doubts" about the final statement, but he is "thinking and acting in the courage of uncertainty." In other words, he does not want to go against the Biblical odds.

But other "liberal" theologians (i.e. those who do not subscribe totally to Biblical literalism) do not experience the same uncertainty about Israel's place in their theology. One of these, probably one of the best known and most influential American Christian theologians of the 1940's and 1950's (at the time of the struggle for Palestine and the early stages of Israel's existence) is Reinhold Niebuhr. Early in his theological career, Niebuhr's emphasis on social analysis displayed Marxist influence. Later he was driven to more theological categories and fell under the existential insights of Kierkegaard and Buber, combined with the rediscovery of the "Biblical View." His understanding of the paradoxes and mysteries of man's historical existence was focused on a set of "Biblical mythical categories."[2] Christian-German guilt feelings are probably responsible for the intensity in which he expresses his Zionist faith and in his becoming an active Zionist propagandist.

Niebuhr's Christian Zionism is based squarely on the "Biblical View": Israel, the old and the new, being a "Biblical category," one of the mysteries of man's historical existence. In an article in the *Nation*, written during World War II,[3] he defended the right of Jews to Palestine as a "collective right." He attacked "modern liberals" because their "individualist and universalist presuppositions and illusions" have prevented them from seeing "obvious facts in man's collective life." The collective will of the Jews, he maintained, requires expression in a homeland for the Jews. Although Niebuhr admonished Zionists for some individual acts of brutality, he could not see that this would diminish their collective right to Palestine.[4] The collective right of Palestinians to their homeland was seldom recognized as an issue, probably because it lacks Biblical foundtions. Or, one might say, because of Biblical foundation, the Palestinians, seen as the modern Canaanites, were dispossessed.

This apparent abandonment of the principle of individual justice (at least in the context of Israel) by some Christian theologians goes against the spirit and the letter of the gospel of Jesus Christ. It reverts to a fundamentalist philosophy based on the Old Testament: the primacy of the collective polity—of a particular tribal collective polity, Israel, the Jewish People.

CHRISTIAN ZIONISTS IN ACTION

In 1942, the leaders of American Zionism decided to marshall the forces of the Christian clergy in the service of their goals—which were then made explicit after the Biltmore Program—of establishing a Jewish State in Palestine. There were many recognized personalities who would be ready to participate. Reinhold Niebuhr, among others, was recruited to help organize the Christian Council on Palestine (CCP). The council's aim was to focus American religious public opinion on the role of Palestine in saving Jewish refugees. Among the members of the executive committee, besides Niebuhr, were such well-known names in American Protestantism as John Haynes Holmes,[5] Paul Tillich, the famous theologian, Daniel A. Poling, editor of the *Christian Herald*, and William F. Albright, the archeologist and Biblical scholar.[6]

The CCP was the result of a meeting of seventy clergymen who formed the "Committee of Christian Leaders, Clergymen and Laymen in Behalf of Jewish Immigration into Palestine." By 1944 the membership in the CCP, which received active financial support from the American Zionist movement, reached 1200 Christian ministers, most of them Protestants. Carl Voss, the Council's secretary, defined its task as enlisting "the aid of ministers in their churches so that the lay constituency of the churches may be urged to action on these important problems affecting Palestine." He then listed four specific subjects of import for the members: 1) The Jewish problem as a Christian problem; 2) The validity of the Balfour Declaration; 3) Opposition of the 1939 British White Paper; and 4) A description of Palestine's development which benefited both Arabs and Jews.[7]

These secular, political issues could become religious concerns of the ministers and their churches only on the premise of the relevance of Biblical texts to the events in Palestine. The link between Zionism and the pro-Zionist Christians was made through emphasis on the Biblical bases of Zionism.[8] The Jewish problem (which is the establishment of a Jewish State at that time) becomes a Christian problem as well. After the establishment of the state ofIsrael this principle was moved one step further. Israel became readily a Christian problem and a Christian responsibility, because it is the fulfillment of Biblical promises.

In 1946, the Christian Council on Palestine merged with another Zionist-supported organization, the American Palestine Committee (which had been formed in 1932 as a primarily secular group supporting the Zionist venture) to form the American Christian

Palestine Committee. More than 3000 American clergymen, over-
whelmingly Protestant, were among its members, and with more
than 100 local chapters organized across the United States. The
total membership of this pro-Zionist Christian organization numbered about 15,000 influential Americans.

In 1943–45 the APC and CCP received from the national American
Zionist Emergency Council the amount of $72,000 per year. By
1947–48 this subsidy rose to $150,000. Local AZEC chapters were
urged to give more in funds and services to the chapters of these
organizations. In answer to charges of being bought by the Zionists,
the executive director of the CCP bluntly stated, "We shall never be
able to secure the widespread Christian support needed for the
fulfillment of the Zionist aspiration unless we have the complete
cooperation of Zionist groups in every community throughout the
United States. . . . Socially sensitive Christians cannot but share a
sense of common guilt for the tragedies and woes of the Jewish
People. Now is the time for them to do something to cure an age old
moral disease in our so-called Christian civilization."[10]

Some of the spokesmen of the organized Christian groups who
supported Jewish migration to Palestine before the establishment
of the Jewish State, were probably under the impression that little or
no hardship would befall the Palestinians. Some were so sensitized
by the plight of the Jews in Europe under the Nazis that they failed to
recognize any Palestinian problem. Niebuhr, however, like many
other religious leaders, was not insensitive to the problem. But he
thought that America should help resettle the Palestinians in the
adjacent Arab land and lend a hand in the creation of an Arab union
or federation "in compensation for the loss of Palestine."[11] Obviously only the Jews deserve a "collective will." Another rationalization
of this imbalance came from S. Ralph Harlow, a professor of religion
at Smith College, who said, at the founding meeting of the CCP, that
"awarding of Palestine to the Zionists involves less of injustice than
any other solution because the Arab countries around Palestine are
crying for larger population." But the guilt feeling among Christians
which was promoted effectively by the Zionists remains the most
probable explanation for this one-sided morality. There is no
matching guilt feeling among Christians towards Muslims, Arabs,
or Palestinians. The Chairman of the CCP, writing in *Christianity
and Crisis* in 1943, argued that helping to make Palestine a "refuge
for the millions of homeless Jews" was not to promote Jewish
nationalism, but rather to provide an "answer to the Christian
problem" of anti-Semitism. "This is not 'Protestant Zionism,' " he
explained. "It is an attempt to answer what is basically not a Jewish

problem but rather a Christian problem."[12]

An important feature of Christian Zionism is represented in these statements. In the thinking of Protestant Zionists there is some divergence on whether the Palestine question is a Jewish concern or a Christian one. There were those who emphasized Jewish needs and those who exaggerated Christian guilt. But very little thought was given to the Palestinians themselves, and no mention at all was made of Islam by this "Judeo-Christian" community, with a "Judeo-Christian" culture.

CHRISTIAN ZIONISM AND THE JEWISH STATE

The Christian Council on Palestine and the American Palestine Committee soon moved from their concern with Jewish refugees to the Jewish Commonwealth after the Biltmore Program in 1942 and the American Jewish Conference in 1943 revealed the true goal of Zionism in Palestine. The National Christian Conference held in Washington in 1946 worked for the merger of the CCP and the APC, in view of the new development, into the American Christian Palestine Committee (ACPC). The Conference exerted great pressure on congressional committees meeting at that time in deliberation of the Palestine Problem.

But the American Christian Palestine Committee, which served for some time the purpose of Zionism before the establishment of Israel in 1948, was losing its relevance in view of the changing emphases of Zionism from a humanitarian concern for the oppressed Jewish refugees to the propagation of the idea of Israel as a political reality. Moreover, the post war period led to the Cold War and the McCarthyist anti-communist fever. The Christian churches, and especially the fundamentalist evangelicals, were up in arms to meet the new danger from the East. While Israel was relatively safe after its victories in 1948, the "Christian soldiers" were mobilized for the defense of the "Israel of the New World" against the hordes of Gog and Magog.

Finally, in the 1950s, the Christian Palestine Committee was exposed as a Zionist front and discredited. During its lifetime, it worked diligently to convince churchmen of Israel's moral and Biblical claims to Palestine. However, the Zionists have been, and still are, active through many other outlets of the Christian establishments. Much of this support, as far as one can determine, is freely given. It emerges from a most basic component within the Christian Church, especially its conservative Protestant (but not exclusively so) branch: the application of literal Biblical text to the situation at hand.

Biblicism, which is widespread among Protestants in England and in America, precedes, in importance and intensity, the guilt complex among Christians and the Christian sense of morality and social justice. These two features were exploited effectively by Zionism before the establishment of the Jewish State. After 1948, and with the realization that some of the guilt feeling and the sense of justice could, and would, be applied to the Palestinians, the Zionists, Jewish and Christian, had to shift their emphasis to the divine selection of Israel and to Israel's centrality in the eschatological economy. This is where the evangelicals can be most effective as tools for Israel in America, as we shall show later. In his testimony before the Anglo-American Inquiry Committee, Reinhold Niebuhr said:

With Israel a reality after 1948, and with the Cold War in the 1950s, Christian Zionism was moving at a slower pace. However, the Franco-British-Israeli attack on Egypt in 1956 was supported by conservative as well as some liberal Christian spokesmen. The thrust was mainly anti-communist and anti-Russian. The Arabs, symbolized by Nasser, were Russian allies, and Israel was valiantly combatting communist infiltration into the Middle East.

Niebuhr again was the Christian Zionist standard bearer in championing Israeli action. Although he did not openly condone the tripartite attack on Egypt, he was incensed because of the "moral complacency of America." He justified the attack by the three nations on Egypt because of their losing confidence in America's "capacity and inclination to protect them against the threat of the new Egyptian dictatorship supported by Russia." He felt it was immoral and futile for America to support the Arabs at the expense of Israel because the "communists have found a way to Nasser's heart through the gift of modern arms."[14] Although he did not express it openly, Niebuhr was Biblical in his linking of the Russians and the Arabs in an "evil" alliance against Israel. Biblical prophecies, according to evangelicals, point clearly to this fact.

ARMAGEDDON APPROACHES

The 1967 war was a turning point for Christian Zionism in America. The obsession with the danger of communism, which had been a very important issue to Christian churches, especially conservatives, was wearing off. The *Six-Day War* was presented as an epic of struggle between good and evil forces. The millennial tendencies among Protestants (and some Catholics) were enormously strengthened. To some, the Six Day War seemed like the beginning of the road to Armageddon. At first, most Israel sympathizers were concerned about the safety of the Jewish State. Prompted by Israeli claims that Israel was fighting for its very life against Arab threats, this danger came as a shock to many Christians who saw in Israel the fulfillment of Biblical prophecy. This was a real challenge to their faith and the veracity of Biblical prophecy; and it put God himself on trial.

Some Christian organizations such as the National Council of Churches and the National Conference of Catholic Bishops remained apparently neutral on this issue. But many other voices outside the evangelical camp were raised in the defense of Israel and in denunciation of the "silent Christians." A. Roy Eckardt, one of Niebuhr's students, was the most active voice among Christian Zionists of this period. Editor of the *Journal of the American Academy of Religion*, and professor of religion at Lehigh University, he echoed the cry of the Zionists in the United States against what he called the silence of the Christian Church towards the attempt by the Arabs to destroy Israel and commit genocide against the Jews. He accused the churches of "murky morality" in refusing to take sides on the Palestine question. He said "the Arabs are wrong in their would-be politicide against the Jewish nation. That policy is not just 'partly' wrong and hence to be only 'partly' opposed; it is altogether wrong and ought to be fought unqualifiedly."[15] He emphasized that the silence of Christians, Protestants and Catholics "amid the Nazi slaughters of the Jewish people" was being repeated in June of 1967.[16] Eckardt's indictment of Christians who do not unqualifiedly support the Jewish State was translated, in a typical Zionist fashion, to a total imputation of the Church. He attributed this "anti-semitism" to the "pathological collective unconsciousness of Christendom, nurtured by centuries of the church's teaching of contempt for Jews."[17]

But Christian leaders accused of neutrality on the 1967 war were not really enemies of Israel. Even those who opposed Israel's expansionism and its treatment of the refugees did always, or almost always, confirm the right of Israel to exist in Palestine. Their commitment to Israel was tempered by a sense of justice that loomed large in their thinking. But Eckardt's outrage, and Niebuhr's justification of Israel's moral right to strike first ("Obviously a nation that knows that it is in danger of strangulation will use its fists.")[18] were expressions of total commitment, a *commitment of faith* demanding complete loyalty. To raise questions about such "absolute truth" amounts to heresy, not merely a difference of opinion. It is this commitment of faith that translates into the "moral commitment" in the American political-religious dictionary.

The Old Testament is centered around the concept of Israel as people and as land, and revolves around the significance of Israel to World History. The New Testament, especially Paul's epistles, supplies some supporting statements to God's choice of Israel the people, but opens that choice to the Gentiles. Still Paul likens original Israel to an olive tree, and the Christians to branches grafted on that tree (Romans 11:24). Christians, therefore, cannot escape confronting the issue of the relevance of the State of Israel to their beliefs. Rejecting any relevance requires strenuous theological exercises. Accepting it, on the other hand, is accepting on faith the authority of the Bible. Either way, Israel is a question of concern to American Christians; their awareness of the Jewish State, its problems, wars, and enemies exceeds that of any country. This condition was created almost automatically as soon as the Zionists decided to call the Jewish State in Palestine by the Biblical name Israel.

Thus, the creation of the State of Israel posed a Christian question and demanded a Christian statement. The Second World Council of Churches meeting at Evanston in 1954 spent much time and energy trying to formulate a resolution on the Christian attitude towards the Jewish State. Political considerations and strong objections from Arab and other non-Western churchmen prevented an all-out statement of support, but they produced no declaration on the irrelevance of the Jewish State to Christian concerns, the Church, or the Scriptures. Recommendations submitted to the Council included such open pro-Israel positions as the following one by the Caucus of the American Committee on the Christian Approach to the Jews:[19]

> The Christian hope cannot be fully comprehended without relation to the hope of Israel, manifested not only in the Old Testament, but also in God's continuous dealings with the Jewish people. The existence of the synagogue and of the Jewish witness to the God of Abraham after 2000 years of church history is a challenge to the church. The church cannot rest until the title of Christ to the Kingdom is recognized by His own people according to the flesh.

In the absence of any statement affirming the theological link between Israel and the Christian Church, a minority declaration, with heavy American representation, was issued. It states:[20]

> We ... believe that God elected Israel for the carrying out of His saving
> purpose. .... Whether we are scandalized or not, that means that we
> are grafted into the old tree of Israel (Rom. 11:24), so that the people
> of the New Covenant cannot be separated from the people of the Old
> Covenant. . . . To expect Jesus Christ means to hope for the
> conversion of the Jewish people, and to love the people of God's
> promise.

This statement contains the essence of the position of conservative
Christians on Israel's relevance to the Church: the connection
between "the Old and the New Covenants," the importance of Israel
for the ingathering and the conversion of the Jews, and the absolute
necessity of all that to prepare for the Coming of Jesus Christ.

THE POLITICS OF ESCHATOLOGY

The theologians, the Christian thinkers, and some Christian
journals such as *Christian Century*, mainly address Christian
intellectuals. In their deliberations about the Palestine problem,
there is some room for disagreement, for give and take. But the
support of Israel among Christian fundamentalists, millenarians,
prophecy groups, and other assorted denominations (referred to
here as Evangelicals) displays an unbending, dogmatic character.
This dogmatic character stems from the basic theological tenet that
Scriptures (Old and New Testaments) are the literal source of their
beliefs, and the final authority on this as well as on any other
question.

Just as fundamentalists still reject categorically the theory of
evolution and strive, in many cases, to eliminate any mention of it in
textbooks, so do they dogmatically assert God's choice of Israel as
His people. Once they were convinced that modern Israel was a
continuation of the Biblical Israel, their commitment to its support
became unlimited, in word and in deed. Thus the evangelicals
became ardent Christian Zionists. Their Zionist creed can be
formulated as follows:

1. All true Christians believe in and expect the Second Coming of
Christ, with ardent hope that this may happen in our lifetime.

2. The establishment of the State of Israel is a "sign" that the
Second Advent must take place soon: the process has already
started. This is based on many, often-quoted passages from both
the Old and the New Testaments.

3. Therefore, any political, economic, ideological, and even military assistance to Israel is good, because it conforms with and hastens the fulfillment of the Advent.

4. Consequently, any opposition to Israel must be against Christianity and against God.

These basic theses of fundamental evangelical Zionism are very well expressed in an advertisement sponsored by more than one hundred churches, mostly Baptist, and published in many newspapers of nation-wide distribution. The ad is one of several, attempting to influence United States policy, after President Carter's statements of support of a Palestinian homeland, and after the joint U.S.-USSR statement in 1977. It is a summation of a wide-spread evangelical campaign. It reads as follows (from the *Chicago Tribune*, July 1, 1976):

> If you want to know where we are in history look at the Jewish people. They are God's time piece and people of prophecy. Part of our eternal clock ticking away as an everlasting reminder that although other peoples or nations may come and go, these people will remain forever. Because that's the way God wants it. Promised it. And planned it. A long time ago.
>
> He made a covenant with Abraham, promising a large portion of the Middle East as an inheritance for him and his descendants. The covenant was unconditional. Just like his love. . . .
>
> This is history today. And as the Jewish people continue to return to their promised land by the thousands, they take part in fulfilling prophecy today. And history tomorrow. Bringing us one step closer to the most important event of all. The return of the Messiah.
>
> Because the Jewish people are the people of prophecy, they are the people of the land. And we knowing Him who made the promise, totally support the people and land of Israel in their God-given, God-promised, God-ordained right to exist.
>
> Any person or group of nations opposed to this right isn't just fighting Israel. But God and Time itself.

The importance of this document lies both in its extreme unconditional faith-commitment to Israel and in the fact that it represents the opinion of a large segment of Christian Americans. It sets the tone that being pro-Israel is not merely a matter of voluntary choice, of humanitarian tendencies, or of political convictions. It is God ordained. To be anti-Israel is almost a cardinal sin. The Baptist and other churches sponsoring the ad range geographically all over the United States and represent a very large membership. The

Southern Baptists alone, not including other Baptist churches, are the largest American Protestant group, with a membership of over thirteen million.

American Zionists certainly appreciate the support they get from this growing movement of Christian Evangelicals, and there is enough evidence pointing out to financial help they give to them. Zionists do, however, regard with suspicion one of the Evangelicals' basic tenets: striving to convert the Jews to Christianity. Thus they resent the growth of the movement of "Jews for Christ," a group of converted Jews who believe that accepting Jesus as the Messiah does not disqualify them as Jews. (In a recent case, the Israeli Supreme Court ruled that conversion to Christianity did indeed disinherit Jews). But Zionists can afford to ignore this little unpleasantness for the wide range of propaganda benefits generated by the religious activities of Evangelicals.

The activities of the Evangelicals in the field of Israel translates into high scores in public opinion polls as well as into votes on the local and national levels. Although they may get some financial help, apparent and hidden, from Zionist circles in support of Evangelical publications, radio and television programs, this widespread campaign, as far as one can determine at present, is largely initiated and financed by contributions from church members and radio and television audiences.

Christian Messianism and millenarianism is as old as, even older than, the discovery of America. The establishment of Israel in 1948, the 1967 and 1973 wars, stirred the fire of prophecy among conservative Christians in America more than any other events since the founding of the Republic. Israel and its wars echo the form and content of Biblical prophecies to those who ardently watch for the Coming of the Lord. Always on the lookout for apocalyptic events to herald the approaching Advent, they find in the "Return of Israel" something to cheer.

The traditional anti-Soviet campaign of the fundamentalists in the late 1940s and 1950s also rested firmly on Biblical prophecy. The focus on Israel in the 1960s and 1970s did not negate or replace the Evangelicals' anti-Russian stand. It actually was a complement to it. The "unfolding" of the drama of the Second Advent involves both the Russians and the Arabs as partners in opposing God's favorite country, Israel, according to scripture-gazers.

Jerusalem plays a most important central role in the hopes of Israelis, Zionists, and Evangelicals. For all of them, although for different reasons, the holy city occupies the center stage of the divine historical drama. Jerusalem, according to the Evangelicals, is the future capital of the world, under the one-thousand-year kingdom of Jesus Christ, after his triumph over the forces of the Anti-Christ in the battle of Armageddon (identified as Megiddo in Palestine). The Biblical prophecies also make it clear, they believe, that the Second Coming is preceded by the rebuilding of the Jewish Temple on the site of the Dome of the Rock and the Al-Aqsa Mosque (Temple Mount). These Muslim shrines will be (or will have to be) destroyed, and the ground returned to its rightful owners, the Jewish people. Most fundamentalists—and some Jews as well—pin their hopes on an earthquake, or some other natural calamity, to take care of the destruction. Some fanatics would like to help Mother Nature and God the Father with acts of sabotage. An Australian Christian fundamentalist, Michael Rohan, in 1969 set fire to the Al-Aqsa Mosque, confessing that he did it to help hasten the coming of the Lord Jesus.

Fundamentalist views of the Evangelicals on the Arab-Israeli conflict are fully treated in a book by William M. Smith entitled *Israeli-Arab Conflict and the Bible* (Glendale, Ca. 1967). The book was inspired by Israel's victory in 1967, and especially by the conquest of Jerusalem. Most of the text is devoted to prove that scriptural Israel is the root of the modern Jewish State, and to the interpretation of current events according to Biblical prophecy. Not until chapter 6 do we find a mention of the Arabs. The author believes they are the enemies of righteousness because they are the enemies of Israel. He does so by equating them with the Edomites who deserved the same title according to the word of God. Thus, he concludes, the Arabs have had "unceasing hatred . . . for Israel down through the centuries."[21]

POPULARIZING ESCHATOLOGICAL ZIONISM

Evangelical fundamentalist literature for popular consumption on the subject of Israel and prophecy is in great abundance. Magazine articles, films, novels, and books on prophecy-analysis reach a great number of the faithful, and hence become politically potent. The best example of the great influence a book can exert on the formation of public opinion, with a pro-Israel perspective, is Hal Lindsey's *The Late Great Planet Earth* (Zondervan, Grand Rapids, Mich.). First published in 1970, it ran through sixty-nine printings by February 1979, with more than ten million copies. This phenomenal success spawned a succession of books on Biblical prophecy, with the same pro-Israel bent, as well as many novels and other related material. Lindsey himself followed his famous book with four more which are but a rehashing of the first one, but with each one going into several printings in relatively short intervals. A motion picture of *The Late Great Planet Earth*, narrated and advertised by Orson Welles, exposed millions more to the same views.

Lindsey does not come with much that is novel in the field of Biblical prophecy. But his explicit identification of Biblical names and symbols with modern countries and events, and his stress on his conviction that Israel is a sure sign of the approaching of the Second Advent, captured the imagination of millions of evangelicals throughout America. He identifies Russia as Gog (Ezekiel 38:17) of Gog and Magog, the sworn enemies of Israel. In chapter six, entitled *Sheik to Sheik*, he does not hesitate in identifying the Arabs, under the leadership of Egypt, as the Biblical "King of the South" who, in alliance with the "King of the North" (Gog or Russia) "will rise up against the restored state of Israel." These two will also be joined by the "Kings of the East" (Revelation 16:12), meaning China, whose army will cross the Euphrates River in order to attack Israel. This Asian horde will wipe out a third of the earth's population (Rev. 9:18) by fire, smoke, and brimstone—prophetic language, Lindsey discovered, for thermonuclear warfare. He further identifies the "Ten Nations," as the countries of the Common Market. These will be ruled by a most powerful dictator who will turn out to be the Antichrist, the Beast, whose number is 666. The Antichrist will make Jerusalem his capital and, at the end of the days, he will be the adversary of the Returning Messiah. The role of the United States in all this is not yet clear. But by being Israel's ally, America is definitely on the right side.

The millennial novels use a very generous dose of this apocalyptic violence, with a sprinkle of clean romance. Such a novel is *They Saw The Second Coming, An Explosive Novel About the End of the World*, by Doug Clark (Harvest House Publishers, Irvine, Ca. 1979). It is a good example of the low level of writing and the abundance of misinformation that are contained in these eschatological novels. The author hosts a television program "Amazing Prophecy" featuring similar information and reaching a wider audience. His utter ignorance about Arabs and Palestinians is exceeded only by his prejudice towards them. (He visited Israel many times). As examples of evil Jew-hating Christians, one of the characters mentions Adolph Hitler and Yasser Arafat (sic), "Neither of those maniacs follow the teachings of the Old or New Testaments." (p. 36) Of the Palestinian "blood-thirsty terrorists" he says: "The PLO are easily identifiable in their white tunics and black turbans." (p. 71) The Old City of Jerusalem had "strange sights and sounds emanating from camels, Arabs, donkeys and exotic looking little bazaars." (p. 127) This and more misinformation about the Arabs are sprinkled all through the novel, together with a great number of Biblical quotations.

According to the plot, America will survive the ravages of Armageddon because it "had preached more Gospel than any other nation . . . and had been a friend to the Jew for a long time." (p. 209) Most of humanity perishes after Armageddon; "the only ones surviving were the people from every nation who had never taken the 'Mark' [of the Antichrist] and who had never hurt the Jewish race." (p. 234)

To the power of books is added that of radio and television broadcasts, widening extensively the outreach of evangelical preaching on behalf of Zionism. Billy Graham is a good example of the new breed of evangelical preachers who use big show-business techniques to reach more souls and more pockets. "Prime-time religion" or "the electronic church" are good money makers. Some examples: The Church of God, one of the oldest electronic churches, gets $65 million annually out of television and radio preaching, the Christian Broadcasting Network makes $25 million, Billy Graham Evangelistic Association $38 million, Praise the Lord Club $25 million, etc.[22] There are at least twenty-five stations almost wholly devoted to religious programming today; almost all of them represent the evangelical point of view, subscribe to the relevance of Biblical prophecy to Israel, and preach Christian Zionism. Complementing the television campaign is a very large number of radio stations found all over the United States to help spread "the word" even further and to bring in the cash in more abundance.

Nationally distributed advertisement in support of Israel, costing thousands of dollars, such as the one mentioned above, are sponsored by evangelical groups in response to Middle East crises. In addition, evangelicals organize events in support of the Jewish State such as the *International Congress for the Peace of Jerusalem* held at Jerusalem in 1978, coordinated by such important evan-gelicals as Douglas Young and Israel Carmona. A group called Evangelicals United for Zion, which began in Philadelphia at a prophecy conference in 1976, distributed awards for those who supported Israel. Billy Graham received the National Interreligious Award from the American Jewish Committee for his "contributions to human rights, the support of Israel, combatting anti-semitism and strengthening relations between Jews and evangelicals." A coordinating group for Christian support of Israel began in the fall of 1978 under the title "International Association of Christians for

Israel" in the state of Washington.[23]

Billy Graham, probably the most famous evangelical (Jimmy Carter, a born-again Christian, now shares the billing) produced one of the most influential religious films, and the most potent, as pro-Israel propaganda. "His Land", viewed by more than 15 million people in America alone, is a religious travelog of the Holy Land. But it contains explicit references to the historic and religious significance of the return of the Chosen People to their Promised Land, and to the great achievements of the Modern State of Israel. The film advertisement proclaims, "The rebirth of the State of Israel . . . is by far the greatest biblical event that has taken place in the twentieth century."

Critics of these evangelical activities charge these groups with "naive Zionism" pointing out that Zionist organizations and Israel are financially behind these actions. There is no doubt about Zionist moral, political and financial support in most of these cases, some of it in the form of advertising in evangelical magazines, arranging for tours to Israel for evangelical groups, and direct payments for expensive advertising in national newspapers. But the fact remains that evangelicals are propagating concepts, beliefs, and political positions that they believe in. Just as it was with the Christian Committee for Palestine in the 1940s, so it is with the evangelical groups in the 1970s: Israel and Zionism are using the Biblicism of Christians for their own ends. Jewish Zionism may have been the midwife, but not the mother, of Christian Zionism.

EVANGELICAL POWER

Evangelicals, an imprecise term that includes fundamentalists, millenarians, and other Biblical literalists, are spread among many Protestant denominations and among Catholics also. They are characterized by a Gallup survey, *Religion in America 1977-1978*,[24] as those who have had "a born again conversion, accept Jesus as . . . personal saviour, believe the Scriptures are the authority for all doctrine, and feel an urgent duty to spread the faith." In other words they are "charged up about their faith." The polls indicate that their number has been steadily increasing, and their activities on the rise. Because of their strict adherence to the letter of the Scriptures, and because of their great emphasis on prophecy, their support for Israel can be taken for granted. Thus, the grass root support for Israel among Americans seems to be steadily increasing, possibly nullifying the effect of the leaning among many liberals for an "evanhanded" position on the Arab-Israeli conflict.

The Gallup poll, admitting that the figures might be low, shows that about 28 percent of Americans, or 40 million adults, are evangelicals. Most of them reside in the South and Midwest. The poll indicates that evangelicals are mostly independent voters. They are therefore "floating voters" whose impact on future elections may be considerable.[25] Most evangelicals are members of the Baptist Church (Jimmy Carter's). But evangelical Christianity has infiltrated most Protestant denominations. Moreover, the poll shows that 20 percent of adult Catholics (or 8 million persons) called themselves evangelicals.

The evangelical spirit is not new in America. The early settlers had millennial ideas. "In revolutionary times, sermons of the ilk of 'The American States Acting over the Part of the Children of Israel in the Wilderness and Thereby Impending their Entrance into Canaan's Rest' (Preached by Nicholas Street in 1777), served to set the millennial tone. . . . Ray Abrams cedits much of the success of the pre-World War I rhetoric of America's clergymen to its millennial urgings."[26] This same spirit moved many preachers to give militant sermons in support of Zionism and Jewish migration to Palestine in the 1930s and 1940s, to heat up the Cold War in fiery anti-Communist sermons in the 1950s, to preach on behalf of America's war in Vietnam in the 1960s, and to return with renewed zeal to championing Israel especially after the 1973 war.

Evangelicals are on the rise. Their number, influence, political clout, and their pro-Israel activities are all increasing. Because America's "moral" and religious commitment to Israel is, to a great extent, built on a strong evangelical (Biblical) foundation, it will not be easily modified by the growing financial and political importance of the Arab World.

Evangelicals believe that their convictions should be translated to action. The following passage explains how the Biblical belief in the "Choice of Israel" should lead to political action on behalf of the Jewish State:[27]

The everlasting promise of God to Abraham, the father of the Jews, "And I will bless them that bless thee, and curse them that curseth thee," implies action—either for or against—the Jews. Supporting the State of Israel is scriptural and humanitarian. And it is one tangible way a Christian can witness to the Jew in this age in which God again is working with Israel in its historic homeland.

"If it is Biblically demonstrated that the restoration of the nation of Israel is in accord with the will and purpose of God," comments Harold Dart, director of the American Christian Committee in Israel, an organization which encourages, among other things, Christian tourism and participation in the reforestation and land reclamation of Israel, "then an evangelical Christian not only can but must take a stand in support of that restoration."

Activism of the evangelicals' pro-Israel stand distinguishes them from most of the Christian liberals who, on either side of the Arab-Israeli conflict, are content with intellectual activities, such as speaking and writing. The program of the evangelical groups calls for, in addition to tourism and land reclamation, the study of Hebrew, contribution for charities in Israel, and missionary work among the Jews. This latter type of activity is the only bone of contention between the evangelicals and the Zionists. But in view of all the other contributions of evangelicals to Israel, evangelical missionarism can be reluctantly tolerated.

The evangelical journal, *Christian Life*, in an issue devoted almost completely to Israel (August 1978), gives a list of activities that the faithful should consider seriously:

1. Join or form a pro-Israel group.
2. Become informed about the Middle East by writing to Israel's Ministry of Information, the Israeli consulates, the local synagogues. (Addresses furnished)
3. Purchase Israel bonds.
4. Write letters to the editors in support of Israel.
5. Buy Israeli products. (List includes Jaffa oranges.)
6. Travel to Israel.
7. Learn Hebrew.
8. Get acquainted with synagogues and the Jewish community.
9. Pray for the peace of Jerusalem.

These recommendations are typical of the fare presented on many radio and television programs dealing with Bible study and with prophecy. From an evangelical point of view, obviously, to them, to God, and to Golda, the Palestinians do not exist.

CIVIL RELIGION IN AMERICA

We have so far explored the religious approach to the Arab-Israeli question from the points of view of two groups of American Protestants. The so-called "liberals", approaching the problem from a Biblical and theological angle, recognize, nevertheless, the pitfalls of offering Israel a complete, unqualified license. They often, but not constantly, concede to a humanitarian consideration of the "Palestinian refugees, and detainees." Although, before the 1940s, some of them did not support the Zionist goal of establishing a Jewish State, preferring a cultural-spiritual home for the Jews in Palestine, they were, after Israel became a fact, converted to the idea that Israel was here to stay.

The conservatives, or evangelicals, approach the question solely from a literal interpretation of the Biblical texts, with special emphasis on the prophetic and apocalyptic perspectives. Their Zionism is purely and directly Biblical and their concern about Israel is an eschatological one.

Both groups have a direct influence on the decision-making apparatus of the U.S. government as voters and constituents, and as pressure groups. But their impact on American foreign policy in the Middle East goes beyond the electoral system and the working of the lobby. It reaches into the formative process of a certain cultural-historical atmosphere in America through Biblical-religious pervasive institutions.

Religion in America is a pervasive institution. As such "it gets mixed up with education, medicine, politics, business, art—there is nothing free from its grasp and grasping. All efforts to fence off certain areas of life from which the church must 'keep out' have been as futile as similar efforts to curtail government or science. Anything can be done religiously, and nothing is safe from ecclesiastical concern. Gone are the days when the salvation of the soul was a distinct and separate business. The separation of church and state does not separate religion and politics, any more than the separation of school and theater separate education and art."[28]

As Bellah put it, "The separation of church and state [in America] has not denied the political realm a religious dimension."[29] Nor, as we see it, has it restricted a political dimension in the religious realm. Israel is a prime example of this mixing of religion and politics in America, and of the potency of this mixture in the field of American foreign policy.

This symbiosis of religion and political institutions in the United States, in spite of the declared principle of separation between Church and State, suggested Robert Bellah, eventuated in a sort of national *shadow religion*, a religion used by the American people to make cosmic sense out of their collective strivings. This is America's *civil religion*, a religion of the body politic using civil-religious rhetoric based on the shared tradition of the three American faiths: Protestant, Catholic, and Jewish.[30]

"The government of the United States and America's organized religious bodies have entered into a very practical compact rooted in an understanding of the role public rhetoric plays in the minds of its citizens and of the stabilizing effect public messages can have on their lives."[31]

According to Herberg, there are three central components, or beliefs, of the American Way of Life, and these beliefs intertwine to make religious pronouncements by American presidents and other political and civic leaders mandatory. Such tenets include belief in God, belief in religion, and belief in the three-faith system: Protestant, Catholic, and Jewish.[32]

Politicians, therefore, must use *rhetoric symbols* which are usually verbalized from a store of religious literature. To keep the three-faith system in America from tension, the only store of religious literature they share is the Old Testament of the Bible, which happens to revolve around the history, the fate, and the moral and civil codes of a people and a land called Israel. Once the connection is made in the public mind between the Biblical Israel and the modern day state of Israel—whether this connection is a direct effect of the name, or a result of a religious or historical conviction— a bias is created and exploited by both the Zionists and the American political establishment.

Protestants especially emphasize the Hebraic roots of their faith. The roots of America's faith are Hebraic. "Its explication was cast in Hebraic metaphors—chosen people, covenanted nation, Egyptian bondage, promised land. Its eager millennial expectation was expressed in the vivid imagery of the Hebrew prophets."[33] To the early colonists and to a large number of American Christians today, America constitutes a new Israel, a land replete with an overwhelming sense of religious destiny—a manifest destiny.

Thus, America's Civil Religion is, in essence, Biblical Religion. And political figures, candidates, senators, and presidents all find it politically expedient to use symbolic rhetoric based on scriptures. When it comes to Israel, the symbols are easily and readily recognizeable in the light of the pervasive influence of the Bible on American cultural and political life.

There is no other explanation that is more satisfactory of the insistence by American politicians that the United States has a "moral commitment to the State of Israel." The exclusive, racial and religious structure of the Jewish State would militate against this "moral" commitment by the United States, devoted to the principles of human rights and the equality of all men, without regard to their race of religion. But the primacy of Biblical standards among religious Americans and the expedient value of Biblical-symbolic rhetoric to the "civil religion" of American politicians override all other considerations.

The term "moral commitment" is used only for Israel and for no other nation. The U.S. may have a "special relationship" with Saudi Arabia, for example, but never a moral one. The relationship with Israel is "for eternity," as President Carter once said. The terms "moral," "eternal," and "Israel" are all rhetorical symbols bridging the gap between the political and the religious realms of the American body politic.

Ever since the Zionists decided to call the Jewish State by the name "Israel" they scored an immediate public relations coup and acquired an instant advantage within the American religio-political system. "Israel" as a Biblical rhetorical symbol has a clear impact on the political position of the American individual on the Middle East. Moreover the emotional-religious character of the word may have a much more effective subliminal influence.

NOTES

1. Richard John Neuhaus. *Christian Faith and Public Policy, Thinking and Acting in the Courage of Uncertainty*, Minneapolis: Augsburg Publishing House, 1977, p. 90.

2. Cf. Langdon Gilkey. "Sources of Protestant Theology in America," in William Gerald McLoughlin and Robert N. Bellah, editors, *Religion in America*, Boston: Houghton Mifflin, 1968, p. 155.

3. Reinhold Niebuhr. "Jews After the War," *The Nation*, February 21, 1942, pp. 214–216.

4. Hertzel Fishman. *American Protestantism and a Jewish State*, Detroit: Wayne State University Press, 1973, pp. 68ff.

5. John Haynes Holmes was a prominent member of an earlier (1930s) pro-Zionist Protestant organization, the Pro-Palestine Federation, financed by Zionists and run by a Jewish executive secretary, Aaron B. Elias. Holmes, a non-denominational Protestant was a supporter of Jewish colonialism in Palestine since 1929. To him the Zionist enterprise in Palestine was "an opportunity to the Jews to build not only for themselves but for all the world an ideal society." John Holmes. "Zion: A Romance and Adventure," in *Pro-Palestine Herald*, Vol. 1, 1932, p. 2.

6. Fishman, op. cit., pp. 72–73.

7. Carl H. Voss. "Christian Ministers Speak Out," in *New Palestine*, March 31, 1944, pp. 339–340. Cf. Fishman, op. cit., p. 73.

8. See H. S. Haddad. "The Biblical Bases of Zionist Colonialism," in *Journal of Palestine Studies*, Vol. III, No. 4, pp. 97–113.

9. Fishman, op. cit., p. 74.

10. Carl H. Voss. "Christians and Zionism in the United States," in *Palestine Year Book* (1946): 497, 500.

11. Fishman, op. cit., p. 74.

12. Henry A. Atkinson. " 'The Jewish Problem' is a Christian Problem," *Christianity and Crisis*, June 28, 1943, pp. 3–4.

13. U.S. Department of State Hearings, as quoted in Fishman, op. cit., p. 79.

14. Reinhold Niebuhr. *Christianity and Crisis*, November 26, 1956, p. 158.

15. A. Roy Eckardt. "Again, Silence in the Churches," in *The Christian Century*, July 26, 1967, p. 973.

16. See also in the same issue of *The Christian Century* (July 26, 1967), David Polish, "Why American Jews are Disillusioned," repeating the same theme of the Eckardt article; "Isaac and Ishmael: 1967," by N. Bruce McLeod, striking a middle-of-the-road position, and "Christians and the Mideast Crisis," by Willard G. Oxtoby, taking a more pro-Arab position.

17. A. Roy Eckardt. "Arab Accusation," *New York Times*, July 13, 1967, p. 36, col. 3 (letters to the editor).

18. Reinhold Niebuhr. "David and Goliath," *Christianity and Crisis*, June 26, 1967, pp. 141–142.

19. Robert Smith. "Israel at Evanston," *International Review of Missions*, 44, 1955, p. 199.

20. *Collection of Statements Made by the World Council of Churches and Representative Bodies of its Member Churches*, Geneva: World Council of Churches, July 1964, p. 15.

21. Wilbur M. Smith. *Israeli-Arab Conflict and the Bible*, Glendale, CA: Regal Books, 1967.

22. See John Mariani. "Television Evangelism: Milking the Flock," in *Saturday Review*, February 3, 1979, pp. 22–25.

23. *Eternity*, January 1978, p. 8.

24. Princeton Religious Research Center, *Religion in America 1977–78*, Princeton, New Jersey, 1979.

25. Ibid. Also *Christianity Today*, January 27,1978, p. 550.

26. Roderick P. Hart. *The Political Pulpit*, Lafayette, Ind.: Purdue University Press, 1977, p. 85.

27. John Chambers. "Should Evangelicals Support the State of Israel?" *Christian Life*, August 1978, p. 30.

28. Herbert Schneider. *Religion in Twentieth Century America*, Cambridge, Mass.: Harvard University Press, 1952, p. 58.

29. Robert N. Bellah. "Civil Religion in America," in *Daedalus*, Winter 1967, p. 3.

30. Bellah's article referred to above created a new concept (Civil Religion) which became the subject of much debate among writers on religious and social topics.

31. Hart, op. cit., p. 46.

32. Will Herberg. "Religion in a Secularized Society: The New Shape of Religion in America," in *The Society of Religion: An Anthology*, ed. by Richard D. Knudten, New York: Meredith, 1967, p. 475.

33. Winthrop Hudson. *Religion in America*, 2nd ed., New York: Scribner's Sons, 1973, p. 112.

8

Christian-Zionist Perspectives on the Middle East.

Larry Ekin

During the 1976 United States presidential campaign Jimmy Carter helped bring the term "born-again Christian" into national consciousness. Since then the terms "born again," "fundamentalist," and "evangelical" have been heard with increasing frequency in the popular media. As a political force many of the groups that have come to be known as the "New Christian Right" gained notoriety especially during the 1980 presidential election, helping to boost Ronald Reagan into the White House. It should be noted that the terms mentioned above are not necessarily synonymous, nor do persons describing themselves in these terms necessarily have the same outlook on all questions. While there are personality and political differences, there has been a political mobilization of many of these persons and groups by leaders working together in an effective coalition.

Pollster George Gallup has compiled the following profile.[1] (1). About one in three Americans acknowledges having been "born again." (2) Thirty-eight percent of the people believe that the Bible is the actual word of God and should be taken literally. (3) Of those who affirm all elements of Gallup's definition (born-again conversion experience, literal interpretation of the Bible, and active personal evangelism) 63 percent are female, 77 percent white, 50 percent live in the South, and 27 percent live in the Midwest.

Research compiled by Jeremy Rifkin and Ted Howard for a recent book provides additional information.[2] (1) Religious book sales constitute more than one third of the total gross sales of the entire commercial book market. (2) In a number of cities proposals are already being developed to build "total church living complexes." These would include "Christian" sub-divisions and apartment complexes, shopping centers, banks, supper clubs, medical offices, and even "Christian" beauty shops and, of course, retirement homes. (3) Approximately 1300 radio stations, one of seven in the United States, is "Christian" owned and operated. (4) The fastest growing segment of private school enrollment is in evangelical schools which already have more than one million students enrolled. On the average two new Christian schools are established every twenty-four hours. (5) Christian broadcasters are adding one new television station to their ranks every thirty days. These now claim a viewing audience of 13 million households, or nearly 20 percent of the entire United States viewing audience. (6) The largest single advertising budget ever put together is represented by Campus Crusade for Christ's proposals to raise one billion dollars to evangelize every man, woman, and child on earth. The Crusade already has more than $170,000,000 on hand.

In terms of what these people believe one finds helpful statements in the *Born Again Catalog*.[3] "But there are certain common convictions which distinguish them from everyone else and give them their special identity." There is a "total commitment to Jesus Christ to achieve salvation"; "He is the *only* way to eternal life"; and the "Bible is inerrant, not only in matters of theological truth, but also in science, or any other subject it may touch upon." The authors of the *Catalog* further assert "born again" Christians are "against premarital sex, adultery, homosexuality, and profanity...," they, "don't drink, smoke, or gamble—though there are exceptions to these standards." These attributes and assertions are not new. Numerous persons who are not "born again" may also agree with some or even all of these ideas. What is new, and what has now attracted hundreds of pages of reports and analyses, is the politicizing of these concerns by crafty organizers from the "New Right." They have found fertile soil in a large body of alienated fundamentalists and evangelicals. The success and popularity of the so-called "electronic church" has helped provide a forum which, coupled with the skillful use of direct mail and energetic organizing efforts has produced the coalescing of the so-called "New Christian Right."

Nowhere is this new confluence of the right-wing with the evangelical movement better illustrated than by the "Religious Roundtable." Formed in September 1979, the Roundtable regularly brings together for strategy coordination representatives of the most influential and financially successful elements of the religious right. A brief examination of some of the members of the Religious Roundtable is illuminating.[4] Ed McAteer was the founder and is often credited with being one of the principal organizing forces behind the new Christian right. McAteer had been the Southeast sales manager for Colgate-Palmolive for twenty-five years. While on the road he had often spent his spare time attending fundamentalist churches, getting to know leading pastors and laymen. When he became a full time political activist as the national field director for the Christian Freedom Foundation[5], his informal network of contacts was most useful. He later became the national field director for the Conservative Caucus and a press contact for the Moral Majority. Articulating his world view, he has said: "I believe there are really two philosophies at warfare, contending for the minds and the allegiances of men." One is the Soviet Union. "On the other side, the philosophy that I adhered to was that of Western civilization, headed up by the United States."[6]

Richard Viguerie, sometimes known as either the "godfather of the New Right" or the "King Midas" of the New Right, is the major fund-raiser for numerous right wing causes. He has helped opponents of the Panama Canal Treaty, of gun control, of busing, of abortion, and of labor law reform. Among his clients are the Conservative Caucus, Gun Owners of America, the Committee for the Survival of A Free Congress, the National Conservative Political Action Committee, and Americans Against Union Control of Government. His organizations pioneered direct-mail fundraising and educational techniques. He employs 300 persons and has put out at least one hundred million pieces of mail, a number he hoped to double in 1981. The sophistication of his operation is illustrated by the fact that his computerized printer can produce two personalized letters a second; that he has a special machine which puts postage stamps on letters slightly crooked, creating the impression that someone sat and licked the stamp on the envelope, and that machines can be programmed to print letters complete with strikeovers and errors, again creating the illusion that someone sat and typed each of the appeals personally. Something else unique about Viguerie's operation is the fact that names developed by his operation remain *his* property rather than the property of the organization that has hired him. This has helped immensely in cross-fertilizing various single issue groups with one another.[7] In addition to Ed McAteer and himself, he has named Howard Phillips and Robert J. Billings as the persons who had designed the strategy for recruiting evangelists into a conservative political movement.[8] The "Christian Voters' Victory Fund" is the lobbying wing of the National Christian Action Coalition which was once the only right-wing religious lobby in Washington.[9] It was headed by Robert Billings who also served as the Executive Director of the Moral Majority until he resigned to serve as Ronald Reagan's religious adviser. The Fund, which shares an office with the Christian Voice, is a political action committee funding candidates it deems "pro-family" and "who believe in the free-enterprise system."[10] Robert Billings is also generally credited with bringing Rev. Jerry Falwell into the movement.

Jerry Falwell is one of the most frequently cited influences behind the New Christian Right. His "Old Time Gospel Hour" broadcasts are carried by more than 600 radio and television stations and reach at least six million persons a week (some estimates are higher). His home church, the Thomas Road Baptist Church of Lynchburg, Virginia, boasts a membership of 17,000. Falwell travels nearly a quarter million miles a year with an entourage (including body-guards) that sometimes numbers fifty persons, including his own 32-member "I Love America" singers. "The Old Time Gospel Hour" employs 90 full-time staff. He has said: "I have a divine mandate to go right into the halls of Congress and fight for laws that will save America. He (God) has called me to take action." He lives on a (modest) $42,500 salary, but he does use church funds for an occasional diversion (like World Series tickets). He has also said: "Material wealth is God's way of blessing those who put him first."[11] The Moral Majority now constitutes the largest of the new lobbying organizations. It has established a goal of organizing chapters in each of the fifty states, though it has acknowledged being well established in only 16 or 17.[12] Before the Reagan election, the Moral Majority's principal work was voter registration, and it claims to have registered three million new voters. In addition to its own $5 million budget, its operations include a Legal Defense Fund and a Moral Majority Political Action Committee to channel funds to conservative candidates.[13]

The "Christian Voice," is a California-based lobbying organiza-tion formed in 1978, with a branch in Washington, D.C., formed in 1979. The organization sends out its "Christian Report Card," ranking legislators on those votes it has decided represent the "Christian perspective." This is mailed to 37,000 pastors from 45 denominations and to 150,000 lay members. The assumption appears to be that the will of God is related to a particular position on a national issue as determined by the organization, and thus the morality of a given congressional representative can be determined by how he or she voted on specific issues. In passing, it might be noted that virtually all the ordained clergymen who were in Congress scored low on this index: Methodist Robert Edgar (Democrat, Pennsylvania) scored 8 percent, Baptist John Buchanan (Democrat, Alabama) scored 29 percent, and Catholic Father Robert Drinan scored zero.[14] In contrast, one of the highest ratings went to Congressman Richard Kelly who was indicted in the Abscam scandal. The Abscam tapes show Kelly stuffing $25,000 into his pockets, then asking the FBI undercover agent: "Does it show?"[15]

Under the direction of Bill Bright, Campus Crusade for Christ has grown from an organization with an $8 million annual budget (1968) to one with more than $30 million annually and 5000 full-time staff at work in 82 countries (1976). In 1977 Bright launched his "Here's Life" campaign, a projected one billion dollar effort to evangelize first the United States and then the entire world. The "Here's Life" campaign is actually part of Bright's "Plan to Save America." An expose in *Sojourner's Magazine* revealed that "Here's Life" was intended to create a grass-roots constituency to elect conservative candidates. Campus Crusade has already raised at least $170,000,000 of the projected one billion. Additionally, Bright was one of the co-chairmen of the April 1980 "Washington for Jesus" rally.[16]

Pat Robertson is president of the Christian Broadcasting Network and host of the "700 Club" television program. CBN is now a $50 million a year operation reaching a potential worldwide audience of 700 million people. Headquartered in their new $50 million complex in Virginia Beach, the 700 Club is aired on nearly 200 television and 150 radio stations in the United States alone. The show has an estimated audience of five million Americans and the capability to reach 86 percent of the television-market households. In addition to his regular broadcasts Robertson makes his thoughts known through the 700 Club newsletter, "Pat Robertson's Perspectives."

Other participants in the Religious Roundtable include: Paul Weyrich (founder of the Committee for the Survival of a Free Congress and another acknowledged major strategist for the "New Right"); Phyllis Schlafly, well-known leader of the Stop ERA (Equal Rights Amendment) movement and founder of the Eagle Forums, the Church League of America (an extremely secretive "research" organization keeping files on thousands of "known communists," as well as "Monitoring communist infiltration of the National Council of Churches, the United Methodist Church, and other church organizations"), Wycliffe Bible Associates, Gideons, Billy

Graham Evangelistic Association (which, it should be pointed out, has distanced itself considerably from many of these organizattions).[18]

While there are differences which merit exploration, these groups agree on far more than they differ. Perhaps the clearest description of their perceived collective purpose came during a "National Affairs Briefing" sponsored by the Roundtable and held in Dallas in August 1980. Over a period of two days fifty speakers in eighteen hours of convention time exhorted the 17,000 participants to:

1. Reject "monkey mythology" by opposing the teaching of evolution in the public schools.

2. "See things in black and white, the way the Scripture does." (Paul Weyrich, director of the Committee for the Survival of a Free Congress)

3. "Not be fooled by the bunk being spread by liberals about the separation of church and state," but to continue demanding that politicians "make decisions based on what God tells us is right." (Governor Fob James of Alabama)

4. Recognize that "America was founded by God." (Guy Vander-Jagt, Republican, Michigan)

5. Give birth to a "Judeo-Christian revolution" to spearhead a "return to soul defense policies" and oppose the "anti-Christ forces of the Kremlin and Peking." (Major-General George J. Keegan, United States Air Force, Retired)

6. Support a constitutional amendment to nullify the Supreme Court decision on abortion.

7. *Support the State of Israel.* (Emphasis added.)

8. See the Equal Rights Amendment "rightfully as the devilish use of one word—'sex' " and understand that the Equal Rights Amendment "does not put women in the Constitution. It puts sex in the Constitution." (Phyllis Schlafly)

9. Hear the "truth" that "the worst thing that has happened to blacks in the past two decades has been white liberalism." (Clay Smothers, Republican, Texas)

10. Remember "some of us here are men of the cloth, some are men of the sword, some men of the republic," but all are "ordained men of the hour" who must "stand for the right in these turbulent days." (Rev. Raymond Barber of Fort Worth, Texas)[19]

One of the most well-received addresses came from the omnipresent Jerry Falwell who urged Christians to oppose abortion, attack pornography, support public school prayer, defeat the Equal Rights Amendment, preserve the free enterprise system, *support Israel* (emphasis added), seek superior national defense, and punish drug pushers.[20]

An analysis of the new right movement was published by *Christian Century* magazine. An article entitled "Christian Politics and the New Right" asserted that there were few philosophical disagreements and that the groups shared several core propositions, including: sin and its symptoms are real; America is suffering from moral decay, the root of which is "secular humanism;" the United States is losing its stature among the nations because of this decay; the prosperity of America is a result of its Christian character. The article concludes: "Next, these interests see the world divided into two main camps. One is the United States and its allies—*including Israel as God's biblically chosen people* (emphasis added)—and the other is the godless forces of communism, which satanically seeks the total overthrow of the United States."[21]

The emphases added in the preceding paragraphs point out an aspect of a phenomenon often overlooked in the multitude of articles that have appeared in the popular media, mainly the explicitly Zionist characteristic adopted by many of the leaders and followers of the New Christian Right. It is not (by and large) a Zionism motivated by love for the Jewish people, nor by guilt over anti-Semitism and the Holocaust. Nor is it even particularly based upon some sort of desire to see that Arabs and Jews work out their problems and live together. It is, rather, a Zionism based upon a particular vision of a theological understanding. The authors of the *Born Again Catalog* assert:

> Finally, most born-again Christians believe strongly that the nation of Israel will play a key role in that final, apocalyptical development of history that culminates in the Second Coming of Christ. As a result, they are very protective of Israel's safety, and can become quite militant in calling for the support of the Jewish homeland."[22]

Pat Robertson (previously-mentioned host of the "700 Club") is known as a strong backer of Israel who opposes the creation of a Palestinian state, or the returning by Israel of any of the territory occupied in 1967. Israel, he says, is "God's favored nation" and the United States should back up this claim.[23] *Sojourner's Magazine* reported the following exchange:

> SOJOURNER'S: You've written you think nuclear war with the Soviet Union is inevitable.
>
> ROBERTSON: I don't think it's inevitable, but I think a war with the Soviet

Union in the Middle East is inevitable if I read Bible prophecy. The
chances are that the United States will come in as a defender of Israel.
It looks like everything is shaping up. The fall of Iran was clearly
foretold in prophecy.[24]

There is not sufficient space here to develop a thorough
understanding of the theological constructions that have led to
these assertions.[25] Briefly, and without discussion of any nuances,
the understanding of these groups is founded upon a belief that
prior to the Second Coming of Jesus Christ there must be an "ingathering," that is a regrouping of the Jews. This must occur in their
Biblical land. They will then be given a final chance to convert to
Christianity ("accept Christ") before the final convulsive apocalyptic shudder of human history, following which Jesus will gather all
true believers with him in heaven.[26] Not all "Christian Zionists" are
motivated by this understanding. As previously mentioned, some
are motivated by feelings of guilt or anguish in relation to the
Holocaust; a few, perhaps, by genuine concern for Jewish people
and a conviction that Israel must exist as the ultimate place of refuge
for victims of anti-Semitism. But the idea of Israel as the fulfillment
of Biblical prophecy remains the predominant expression of supporters constituting the New Christian Right.

There are numerous other manifestations of evangelical and/or
fundamentalist support for Israel stemming from these ideas.
Fifteen major American evangelical leaders signed full-page ads in
the *New York Times* and the *Washington Post* which stated: "We
believe the rebirth of Israel as a nation and return of her people to
the land is clearly foretold in the Bible, and this fulfillment in our
time is one of the momentous events in all human history."[27] One of
the most interesting developments has been the establishment of an
"International Christian Embassy" in Jerusalem during the last
week of September, 1980. Located on the same street as Jerusalem
Mayor Teddy Kollek's home, the "embassy" has a full-time staff of at
least twenty from nine different countries, and it was set up to "aid
pilgrims, operate a public relations bureau and work with Christian
groups abroad to sell Israeli products."[28] It was established partially
in response to the withdrawal from Jerusalem of thirteen govern-
mental embassies, but also because its leadership believes: "Passive support for Israel is not enough, we believe in action. You seek
aid from 7 million Jews—but there are 70 million Christians waiting
to be exploited."[29] A spokesman continued: "You can see us as a
kind of Jewish Agency."[30] A *Jerusalem Post* article concludes: "The
embassy promotes every kind of propaganda for the cause it

cherishes, through press, radio, films, tapes, meetings, 'love-Israel' nights."[31] They have also been active in trying to help the Israeli economy by promoting the sale of Israeli goods. And, says embassy spokesman Jan Willem van der Hoeven, a Dutchman, "If only Israeli guides acquire the habit, while taking Christian groups to the Israel Museum or wherever, of making a 15-minute stop at the embassy, we'd give them an idea of what we're trying to do."[32]

Yet another Christian fundamentalist effort in the region can be seen just across the Lebanese border. Planted firmly in the tiny strip of territory controlled by Israeli ally Saad Haddad, the Christian radio station "Voice of Hope" broadcasts its daily mix of American country-western and gospel music with Bible lessons and Haddad propaganda. The station represents an initial investment of $600,000, much of it raised with help from fundamentalist entertainer Pat Boone. It uses two solid-state transmitters of 15,000 watts each (in case one gets knocked out), has its own generators for power, and can reach as far as Iran and Saudi Arabia. Behind the station is an organization based in Van Nuys, California, "High Adventure Ministries," whose founder, George Otis, is a former general manager of the Lear Jet Corporation. In response to protests from the Lebanese government, newspapers, the Middle East Council of Churches, the United States Council of Churches regarding the political consequences of the station's broadcasts, and to charges that the station is merely a propaganda vehicle for Haddad, Otis explained that letting Haddad use the radio was like paying him rent for the station and the land. Haddad's spokesman was the station's news director. Otis said, "If Major Haddad wants to make an announcement over the air or comfort his people, he's earned it. I don't understand Arabic so we don't know what he's said and it's none of our business," he added.[33] In March, 1981 the organization also began conducting television broadcasts from within the Haddad enclave.[34]

These activities have not gone unnoticed by the Israeli government and other Zionist leaders. On April 14, 1980 Israeli Prime Minister Begin, while staying at Blair House in Washington, D.C., held a private meeting with eight United States evangelical leaders including Jerry Falwell. It ended with Falwell reading a letter: "We proclaim that the Land of Israel encompasses Judea and Samaria (Mr. Begin's preferred terms for the West Bank) as integral parts of the Jewish patrimony, with Jerusalem its one and indivisible capital. Israel stands as a bulwark of strength against those, who by terror and blackmail threaten our democratic way of life."[35] Falwell was one of the first recipients of the recently-created "Jabotinsky

Award" created by the Begin government to honor persons who have done outstanding work for Israel. And, when the Israeli government bombed the Iraqi nuclear reactor, Jerry Falwell received an urgent phone call from Menachem Begin who asked Falwell to "explain to the Christian public the reasons for the bombing."[36]

The annual "Jerusalem Day" parade is the Israeli commemoration of the "unification" of the city during the 1967 War. Next to Israeli Independence Day, it is perhaps the major nationalist celebration. In 1980 it included 12,000 civilian and 35,000 military marchers. One thousand of the civilians were representatives of Christian fundamentalist groups. A Christian Zionist writing a guest column in the *Jerusalem Post* observed: "Participating in the annual Jerusalem March, the Christians were greatly honoured by being placed just behind the Israeli Army's leading contingent."[37]

In a story highlighting these relations, the *Washington Post* quoted an aide of Prime Minister Begin as saying the evangelicals "are a pillar that Israel has in the United States. They number 10 times the Jews in America, and they are outspoken. Naturally, we look kindly on what they are doing." The article further noted that Israeli officials considered the principal question to be how this support would be translated into practical terms: "through lobbying and other forms of pressure such as those exercised by the Moral Majority during the last United States election campaign—and what effects it will have on Reagan administration policies."[38]

While many American Jews appreciate the support for Israel voiced by the "New Christian Right," many are also inclined to view the movement with a certain ambivalence. There have been suspicions and charges of anti-Semitism. Rabbi Alexander Schindler has argued: "After all, the deepest reasons for the support given to Israel by the evangelical fundamentalists are theologically self-serving. As *they* (emphasis original) read the Scripture, Jesus cannot return for the Second Coming until all the Jews are regrouped in the whole of their Biblical land and are then converted to Christianity. . . . This is their apocalyptic vision in all its fullness: they seek our extinction as a particular people."[39] Suspicions were sharpened after Rev. Bailey Smith, head of the 13 million-member Southern Baptist Convention, commented that "God Almighty does not hear the prayer of a Jew."[40] Jerry Falwell has been quick to repudiate charges of anti-Semitism. In addition to citing his reception of the Jabotinksy Medal, he has asserted: "There is not one anti-Semite in a Bible-believing church in America," and "God has blessed America because America has blessed the Jew."[41]

However, in an analysis published by *Chistianity and Crisis*, the theologian Robert McAffee Brown pointed out:

> Has America really 'blessed the Jew'? I would rather hear the answer from a Jew than from a Southern Baptist. And Jews who take this statement as a sign of openness to dialogue and sharing need to read elsewhere, for Falwell frequently states that another reason God has blessed America is that America is 'the last logical base for world evangelism.' Jews had better beware that 'world evangelism' on the fundamentalist lexicon is dedicated to fashioning a world in which there will be no more Jews.[42]

There have been numerous other voices raised in opposition to the doctrines of the "New Christian Right." According to a November 13, 1981 story in the *United Methodist Reporter*, Syrian Orthodox Archbishop Mar Ignatius Zakka I speaking in New York "complained here that convert-seeking evangelicals who militantly support Israel are creating problems for Christians in the Middle East." Others, of all different faiths and a variety of political perspectives, have likewise challenged the peculiar wedding of politics and theology of the "New Christian Right." Theologically, it has been argued they are shallow and completely ahistorical (seldom, if ever, do they put Scriptural references into a proper historical/cultural context); extremely selective in their interpretation (there is seldom mention, for instance, of the Old Testament emphasis on justice and the necessity of establishing just relations with one's neighbors); and simplistic. Politically, critics have pointed out that they represent a threat to a pluralistic society and that many of their positions stem from an economic analysis which is merely a passionate embrace of the myths surrounding free enterprise capitalism.

As of this writing, the "New Christian Right" shows no signs of either disappearing or dissolving into factional warfare. Flushed with victory, a group of 2500 evangelical leaders met in the wake of the Reagan inauguration to evaluate their performance and plan their strategy for the 1980s. Their confidence was summarized by Bobbie James, the wife of Alabama governor Fob James: "It was Jesus that gave us this victory in November—God in his mercy heard the prayers of Christians all over this country . . . perhaps all over the world."[43] Such confidence will certainly carry them into the 1982 elections and beyond.

NOTES

1. William Proctor. *The Born Again Christian Catalog: A Complete Sourcebook for Evangelicals.* New York: M. Evans & Company, Inc., 1979, pp. 8–9.

2. Jeremy Rifkin and Ted Howard. *The Emerging Order: God in the Age of Scarcity.* New York: G. P. Putnam's Sons, 1979. Portions summarized in *In These Times, Chicago, Weekly.* January 8, 1980 edition. Also, *Press On!,* Winter, 1980 edition. Quarterly publication of the World Student Christian Federation: North American Region.

3. Proctor, op. cit., pp. 1–7.

4. Deborah Huntington and Ruth Kaplan. "Whose Gold is Behind the Altar? Corporate Ties to Evangelicals," *Press On!,* World Student Christian Federation, Volume 2, Number 1. (Hereinafter, Huntington and Kaplan.)

5. Peggy L. Shriver. *The Bible Vote.* New York: The Pilgrims Press, 1981. p. 12. (Hereinafter, Shriver)

6. "Roundtable's President Ed McAteer is Music Man of Religious Right," *Conservative Digest.* January, 1981.

7. Nick Kotz. "King Midas of 'The New Right.' " *Atlantic Monthly,* November, 1978. Frances Fitzgerald. "The Triumphs of the New Right," *New York Review of Books,* November, 19, 1981.

8. Shriver, p. 11.

9. Ibid., p. 11.

10. Huntington and Kaplan.

11. *The Indianapolis Star,* July 14, 1980. *Time,* September 15, 1980. *Newsweek,* November 10, 1980.

12. *Wall Street Journal,* February 12, 1981.

13. Huntington and Kaplan.

14. *New York Times,* August 17, 1980.

15. Huntington and Kaplan.

16. Ibid.

17. "Pat Robertson's Politics," *Sojourner's Magazine,* September, 1979.

18. Huntington and Kaplan.

19. *United Methodist Reporter,* Weekly. August 29, 1980 edition. *United Methodist Reporter,* Weekly. September 5, 1980 edition.

20. Ibid.

21. Proctor.

22. Ibid., pp. 2–3

23. "Pat Robertson's Politics," *Sojourner's Magazine,* September, 1979.

24. Ibid.

25. One of the best discussions of the theological basis of the fundamentalists is found in the volume by Dr. Dewey M. Beegle, *Prophecy and Prediction.* Ann Arbor: Pryor Pettengill, 1978. Dr. Beegle is a professor of Old Testament at Wesley Theological Seminary in Washington, D.C. A shorter discussion, still extremely illuminating, was published by *Sojourner's Magazine,* March, 1977. It is entitled "The Promise and the Promised Land."

26. Christian Zionist publications including: "Jerusalem My Chosen," Pembroke Pines, Florida: Peace for Israel, Inc. Jack Van Impe. "Israel's Final Holocaust." Royal Oak, Michigan: Jack Van Impe Ministries. Institute

of Holy Land Studies, various publications, Highland Park, Illinois and Jerusalem. Messianic Life Ministries, various publications, Bedford, Texas and Jerusalem. Evangelicals United for Zion, various publications, Lakehurst, New Jersey.

27. Proctor.
28. *Jerusalem Post International Edition*, October 5–11, 1980.
29. Ibid., August 2–8, 1981.
30. Ibid.,
31. Ibid.
32. Ibid.,
33. *IKE*, English Language Daily, Beirut. August 28, 1979. August 31, 1979. September 2, 1979.
34. *United Methodist Reporter*, weekly. November 13, 1981.
35. *Moral Majority Report*, May, 1980.
36. *Moral Majority Report*, July 20, 1981.
37. *Jerusalem Post International Edition*, October 12–18, 1980.
38. *Washington Post*, March 23, 1981.
39. Shriver, p. 70.
40. *New York Times*, December 14, 1981.
41. Allen Hunter. "In The Wings," *Radical America*, Spring, 1981.
42. Robert McAffee Brown. "Listen, Jerry Falwell!" *Christianity and Crisis*, December 22, 1980, p. 364.
43. Marjorie Hyer. "Evangelical Christians Meet to Develop Strategy for 1980s," *Washington Post*, January 30, 1981, p. C14.

OTHER SOURCES

New York Times. August 18, 19, 21, 1980.
Sojourner's Magazine. "Evangelical Zionism," May, 1979. "Biblically Buttressed Land Grab," July, 1979.
New York Magazine. "Pray TV," October 6, 1980.

The most comprehensive collection of articles on the "New Right" can be found in an excellent four volume survey organized and published by: The Data Center, 464 19th Street, Oakland, California, 94612, Phone: (415) 835-4692. It should prove an indispensable tool for authors and researchers.

9

Impacting United States Church Policies
on the Middle East

Beth E. Heisey

Years ago a Syrian woman named Mrs. Wahad Nassif sent a letter
to Dr. William Thompson, then President of the National Council of
Churches. Refusing to leave her ruined city, Qnaytra, after its
destruction following the October 1973 war, she wrote as follows:

Dear Dr. Thompson,
    . . . I am a Presbyterian Christian 72 years old who went through the
Palestinian situations and the Qnaytra occupation by the Israelis and
the willful destruction of the bountiful and unique city of Qnaytra.
    We Arab Christians have been most surprised that the American
Christians have not taken more interest in our plight and our human
rights.
    The Protestant Church has taken interest in human rights all over
the world except our part of the world. . . .
    I hope you will turn your Christian kindliness towards us.

Sincerely,

Wahad Nassif[1]

In her own small way, Mrs. Nassif, through her letter, was crying out
to the American church, chiding it for its oversights and encouraging it to respond more forthrightly to the plights she had experienced. Arab Americans who likewise wish to communicate with
U.S. church leadership or impact any formulated Middle East
policies must follow the lead of Mrs. Nassif and address the

American church in a systematic and comprehensive manner. Towards that task, this paper will attempt to 1) examine the nature and strength of the organized church in America, 2) evaluate existing church policies on the Middle East, and 3) enumerate specific suggestions for affecting the churches' stance at local, state, and national levels.

THE NATURE OF THE ORGANIZED CHURCH IN THE U.S.

The 1980 Presidential elections are a recent illustration of the powerful impact churches can exercise over U.S. affairs. To fully fathom the extent of this impact, however, we need to understand what gives the church this power.

First, there are the sheer numbers. According to the *1980 Yearbook of American and Canadian Churches*, approximately 60% of the American population, or 127 million, are church members. Of this figure, 73 million are Protestants, 50 million are Roman Catholics, and more than 3½ million belong to Eastern Churches (Orthodox). These Christians worship in 300,000 Protestant churches, 25,000 Roman Catholic, and 1500 Eastern churches, respectively. 5.7 million Americans are listed as members of Jewish congregations.

Secondly, there is no doubt the Church in America wields substantial economic power; it is a tax-exempt, multi-billion-dollar industry. Contributions in 1980 alone by church members of 44 communions (out of 222 recognized U.S. religious bodies) totalled more than $8 billion dollars.[2] In addition, religious institutions received more than $20 billion dollars from foundations, corporations and the American public for charitable purposes. Aside from contributions, more opportunities for the individual Christian to spend his/her own money have arisen as the church has become more secularized. There are 52 different English translations/paraphrases of the Bible, for example, so that many Christians buy 2 or 3 versions for individual needs. One of the most popular paraphrased Bibles, *The Living Bible*, sold 23 million copies in one edition alone.[3] And then there are all sorts of study aids, devotional books, cassettes, calendars, concordances, and Bible almanacs available for purchase. For entertainment, one can purchase the latest "Best Selling" Christian record or read the latest "Best Selling" book. One book which has consistently placed high in the charts is entitled *The Late, Great Planet Earth*, an outline of the "End Times" based on the Evangelical, pre-millennialist interpretation of Old Testament prophecies, and a book that has shaped many a Christian's attitude toward Israel, the U.S.S.R., and the Arabs. To date this book has sold 10 million copies. Recently, however, it has started receiving stiff competition from John Walvoord's *Armageddon, Oil and the Middle East Crisis.*[4] One of the fastest growing businesses in the U.S. currently is Christian radio and television broadcasting. More than 1,000 Christian radio and 24 TV stations now exist across the country. Millions of dollars are being spent by this "electronic church" and millions more are being received from audiences which now stretch around the globe. Many of the programs are stridently pro-Israeli and anti-Arab.[5]

A third reason for the Church's influence is that it controls the institutional structures needed to reach large numbers of people. Not only does it possess the formidable radio and television networks already mentioned, but it prints thousands of newsletters, periodicals, and other literature in its publishing houses, disseminating information to respective constituencies and encouraging action on selected issues. This fact was greatly appreciated during the Presidential campaign as each candidate courted religious leaders as assiduously as labor and business leaders.

Fourthly, the Church has always played a major educational role in American society. It owns and administers hundreds of colleges and universities and seminaries as well as countless private schools for children. In addition, Sunday morning services, Sunday School curricula (for children and adults), films, conventions, and special events provide extensive opportunity for influencing opinions, inculcating values, and directing behavior.

Fifth, the Church is perceived as a major moral and spiritual force. Despite apparent secularization of American society, the Church continues to enjoy a large degree of public confidence and can speak with moral authority on the issues of the hour.

The Church's power is particularly significant on issues relating to the Middle East. Christianity has Jewish roots and originated in the Middle East. Old Testament scriptures are filled with the history of the Hebrew people's sojourn in Palestine, the wars of the ancient Kingdom of Israel, and the special dealings of God with the "chosen people." Hymns, weekly sermons, and scripture readings make constant reference to this history and surround it with a special halo of recognition and identification. The political effect is devastating, however, when the lines of distinction begin to blur between the religious, spiritual, historical references and the modern, secular realities and events. Israelis become confused with the ancient Israelites; Palestinians somehow are equated with the evil Philistines; the modern secular State of Israel is a reincarnation of the old theocracy striving to do God's will in a hostile environment. Yet the transposition of concepts and attitudes inherent in this 2000-year leap is rarely challenged. On the contrary, it is often reinforced and encouraged in everything from Holy Land Tours to church curricula.[6]

CHURCH POLICIES REGARDING THE MIDDLE EAST

There is no unified position maintained by American Christians on the Middle East. There are discernible viewpoints, particularly in evidence when comparing the stances generally held by the membership of Evangelical vis-à-vis "mainline" churches. Official church positions take the form of policy statements or resolutions.

The policy statement which received the most media attention within the past year is the one passed unanimously in November, 1980 by the National Council of Churches of Christ/USA (hereafter referred to as NCC). That this statement received a lot of attention, both during and after its formulation, is no surprise. NCC is the largest ecumenical body in the United States, with its 32 member Protestant and Orthodox communions representing 40 million Americans. Official representatives from these 32 member bodies are chosen to serve on the Governing Board and it is this Board which issued the statement, 3 years in the making.

In struggling to update its previous policy, NCC created a panel of high-level officers for a fact-finding tour of the Middle East and published a study document reporting on that trip. This document reflects the 5 major areas of concern by the panel: 1) Security in the region, 2) the right of Palestinian Arabs to self-determination, 3) Human Rights issues, 4) Settlements on the West Bank, and 5) Religious issues.[7] With the development of the Study Document, the NCC decided to hold open Congressional-style hearings for interested parties as well as less formal meetings with Jewish and Arab American spokesmen. Lobbying by American Jewish organizations and individuals was intense and persistent, commensurate with the perceived impact the NCC Statement would foster. By comparison, pressure during the above process from the American Arab community, though welcomed by NCC, was minimal.

The policy statement resulting from all the collective work took a definite stand, inter alia, on the Israeli-Palestinian conflict. It calls on Israel to recognize the "right of Palestinians to self-determination, including the option of a sovereign state apart from the Hashemite Kingdom of Jordan and of its acceptance of the PLO as a participant in the peace negotiations." Further, the document reads, steps toward peace must include PLO recognition of Israel as a sovereign state and its right to continue as a Jewish state. In the meantime, each party to the conflict should refrain from all hostile acts against the other. Unilateral actions in respect to settlements and land and water use in the occupied areas are seen to "only inflame attitudes and reduce the prospect of achieving peace." Provision for solutions to problems of all refugees and displaced persons as a result of the conflict since 1948 must be made, including questions of compensation and return.[8]

As with any major action by NCC, information and attendant materials were distributed to press, to local and state Councils of Churches across the country, and to the administrative offices of each of its 32-member communions, to be filtered in turn to each respective constituency. Plans were made for follow-up action, to include attempts to bring together Jewish and Palestinian leaders to discuss the report and dissemination and discussion of the document/study guide with State Department and Congressional personnel.

But the National Council of Churches is not the only group to form resolutions around Middle East developments. The U.S. Catholic Bishops also issued a statement on the Middle East. While lauding the Camp David accords as a courageous step toward peace, that statement was careful to define its limits—failure to "bring key actors into the peacemaking process" and resolve satisfactorily the status of Jerusalem and the fate of the Palestinians. This statement also devotes more attention than any other to the conflicts in Lebanon ("The independence of Lebanon and its fabric of political and religious pluralism must be preserved. We call upon our government to have a special concern for all these elements."). It also reiterates its 1973 position on the rights of Israel to exist as a sovereign state within secure and recognized boundaries as well as the rights of the Palestinian Arabs to participate in negotiations affecting their destiny, and to a homeland of their own. Just compensation should be provided for all parties concerned and the status of Jerusalem should be "preserved through an international guarantee of access to the holy places and the preservation of a religiously pluralist citizenry."

While specifics of other resolutions can be enumerated at length, individuals desiring more complete information may contact the other religious bodies which have formulated Middle Eastern positions: The United Church of Christ, the Vatican, Reformed Church in America, American Baptist Churches, the United Methodist Church, Church of the Brethren, United Presbyterian Church, the Antiochian Orthodox Church, and the World Council of Churches (the largest ecumenical organization, composed of 295 Protestant, Anglican, Orthodox, and old Catholic churches in more than 90 countries.)

Generally speaking, the consensus exhibited in these policies is that there are two distinct peoples involved in the Middle East conflict, Israelis and Palestinians; that each is entitled to self-determination; and that in order for this to be realized mutual compromise between both parties must take place. Thus the official stance of the PLO is regarded as untenable as is the current Israeli refusal to return to pre-1967 borders. Much emphasis is given to the importance of a peaceful solution to conflicts in the Middle East through dialogue; the need for study, reflection and action on the part of American Christians; an appreciation for the role of the United Nations; the necessity of preserving the international character of Jerusalem; an increasing awareness of the danger of military build-up in the region and U.S. complicity in this; and some new introspection regarding the prejudicial nature of American Christian attitudes toward Middle Eastern peoples—the latter acknowledgement surfacing in reaction to the mistreatment of Iranian students in the U.S. following the overthrow of the Shah. No mention is made of harassment or mistreatment of Arab students.

One may be tempted, after all is said and done, to toss Church resolutions into the same wastebasket as United Nations resolutions. However, to the extent that these declarations reflect the views of a particular communion and stimulate specific actions, they are valuable. Resolutions also serve as an instrument by which the Church can speak out on matters of international concern and justice. They serve as the parameters within which church leadership can officially respond to developments/crises in the Middle East, they are an indicator of the fact that there are Christians who work hard at understanding the Middle East in more than a superficial way, and they are a concrete way to express solidarity, educate constituency, and stimulate public discourse.

One danger that the activist must avoid is to think that his task is to produce more and more favorable church statements on the Middle East. It must always be remembered that there may be a gap between the church leadership/staff who draft the statements and the average church-goer. Efforts to influence the Church's position are best directed at the Christian on the grassroots level as much as at those in leadership and must provide a base of support and implementation of favorable policy statements.

IMPACTING CHURCH POLICIES

Stances of American church-goers have generally evolved without benefit of access to the Arab point of view; they are often based on false assumptions, bias, misinformation, or plain ignorance. The following are suggestions of ways to correct this situation, whether reflected in the average church-goer's opinions or official church resolutions.

1) Inform yourself about the Church. An excellent basic reference for your perusal is the *1981 Yearbook of American and Canadian Churches*. It will give the reader a concise, bird's-eye-view of churches in America, cooperative church agencies, international relief organizations, councils of churches, and church-related institutions of higher education. All of this information is complete with addresses, names of the officials of each organization, and its historical/theological orientation. In addition, the top 200 church, Jewish, and Muslim periodicals are listed with names and addresses.

A second part of the task involves familiarization with the local churches where you live.

2) Target a particular church, denomination, seminary or church-related organization. If you decide to work with a particular church, check if it is part of the National Council of Churches (if so you can work with its delegate(s) to the NCC Governing Board). Otherwise, find out if your church has an official position on the Middle East. Again, keep in mind that there is often a marked difference between the official position of a church body and that of a specific congregation or its pastor.

3) Check existing and available channels. Determine if there is an ecumenical officer or Interfaith Task Force whose job it is to be sensitive to interfaith concerns. Find out if there is a committee for dealing with social or current political issues. Sometimes there is a "missions night" or other special program or activity where outside speakers are sought to address the congregation. If the church has a magazine or newsletter, consider submitting an article on such topics as indigenous Christians in the Middle East, Islam, oil, a current Middle East topic, the Jerusalem Law, peace and justice in the Middle East, or a human interest story.[9]

4) Initiate contact and make yourself available. There is a great deal of interest and curiosity on the part of the church members regarding the Middle East. One must take the initiative, however. The mere fact that one is an Arab or a Muslim is sufficient to arouse the interest of a church audience. One Palestinian college student

supplemented his income by showing "Holy Land" slides and giving speeches in churches in the region where his college was located. At the very minimum, he humanized the Middle East conflicts for many and destroyed some commonly-held myths (e.g. all Arabs are Muslims; all Palestinians are terrorists; Jericho and Bethlehem are Israeli towns).

Availability includes being open for human contact, not just political indoctrination. There is as much value in American Christians experiencing Arabs as human beings as there is in extensive cultural/political/social education on the Middle East.

5) Be sure to gear your presentation to your audience. It is a cardinal rule that one should constantly keep his/her audience in mind. This is particularly true when a stranger confronts an American audience and attempts to influence its views. A few hints on addressing a church audience may be helpful:

a) Target issues of peace, justice, theological importance.

b) Humanize the situation and analogize it to enable your audience to understand you. Employ personal references as appropriate.

c) Avoid unnecessary complexities and answer questions or concerns that are raised in a direct manner.

d) If you know your Bible, quote it. Many of the teachings, especially of Old Testament prophets, are effective if correctly used.

e) Avoid becoming argumentative or rhetorical. Stick to the facts.

f) Do *not* assume anything, however obvious it may be to you. Be prepared to start from the very basics. Many are not familiar with the geography of the region. Fewer possess a working knowledge of Islam or know that there are Arab Christians. *Do* assume that you have something to contribute to any church audience and that many are eager to listen to what you have to say about "an issue we feel is too complex for us to ever understand."

g) Challenge your audience to live up to their Christian values and responsibilities, as did Mrs. Nassif.

h) Do not glorify "the gun." Acknowledge the brutality of war for anyone and the evil of arms buildups.

i) Practice the art of "listening."

j) Be honest. Do not exaggerate. Do not hesitate to admit errors committed by Arabs or Arab governments. Remember that a speaker's tone, manner and credibility are at least as important as the substance of what is said.

k) Familiarize yourself with the Evangelical positions on prophecy and the Biblical counter arguments. It will not suffice to dismiss ingrown doctrines such as "God's chosen people" or "return to the land of Israel" without offering religious/theological rebuttal.[10]

l) If you discover prejudice against Jews, do not promote your case by building on it. Rather, challenge this attitude and present the Arab case on its own numerous merits.

6) Cooperate with others. While it is important for each to start where he is geographically and in light of personal abilities, interests, and resources, the task is large and calls for concerted cooperation. Efforts must be made by the Arab Christian and Muslim communities to address the Church directly. Church publications can be monitored and material prejudicial to Arabs or racially biased must be challenged directly. Letters to editors and personal visits or phone calls must be utilized to point out flagrant misrepresentations in church publications. Good use of free television time for the public for local religious programming should be made. Seminars can be organized. Trips to the Middle East can be sponsored for selected individuals. The opportunities for joint action are many.

In summation, the task of addressing the American Church, in general, and its positions on the Middle East, in particular, is large, but not hopeless. Action on the part of the American Arab community is vital to this task. It is hoped that through the efforts of many people like Mrs. Nassif more of the American Church will take steps to discover what shape its commitment to peace and justice in the Middle East must take.

NOTES

1. Wahad Nassif letter of April 25, 1977 from the files of Dr. Frank Maria, Antiochian Orthodox Christian Archdiocese delegate to NCC.

2. *1981 Yearbook of American and Canadian Churches*, edited by Constant Jacquet, Jr., Nashville, Tennessee: Abingdon Press, p. 241.

3. *The Born-Again Christian Catalog: A Complete Sourcebook for Evangelicals*, William Proctor, New York: M. Evans and Company, Inc., 1979, p. 232.

4. Survey of "Best-Selling Christian Books," Monthly lists for February-October 1980 in *Bookstore Journal*. Provided by Christian Booksellers Association, Co.

5. Richard M. Harley, "The Evangelical Vote and the Presidency," *The Christian Science Monitor*, Wednesday, June 25, 1980, pp. 12-13.

6. See, for example, the 1978 brochure printed by Wholesale Tours International (387 Park Avenue South, New York, NY 10016) entitled "Scripture Referencs." This brochure, included in packets of information for prospective organizers of Holy Land Tours, is intended to appeal to Christians who can, at a glance, see lists of scripture (naming places where various events took place) under their corresponding countries. So, scriptures naming Tyre and Sidon are grouped under "Lebanon." Scriptures, however, naming Jericho, Bethlehem, the Jordan River and Jerusalem, among others, are all grouped under the heading "Israel."

7. *Middle East Panel Report: A Study Document*, National Council of the Churches of Christ, USA, June 1980. Copies available from the national office at 475 Riverside Drive, New York, NY 10115. $2.00 each/$1.75 for quantities of five or more.

8. *Middle East Policy Statement*, Adopted by The Governing Board, National Council of Churches of Christ in the U.S.A., November 6, 1980. Available free of charge from National Council of the Churches of Christ in the U.S.A., 475 Riverside Drive, Room 880, New York, NY 10115. For a more comprehensive look at the process surrounding the development of this statement, see *The Link*, Vol. 13, No. 5, December 1980, published by Americans for Middle East Understanding, Inc., Room 771, 475 Riverside Drive, New York, NY 10115.

9. See "Ten Things I Wish North American Mennonites Knew About My People," by Elias George, *Festival Quarterly*, November, December, 1979, January 1980 issue, p. 15. (His photograph was used to grace the cover of the magazine.)

10. Recommended reading is the book *Prophecy and Prediction* by Dewey M. Beegle, Pryor Pettengill, Ann Arbor, MI, 1978 or his article "The Promise and the Promised Land," *Sojourners*, March 1977, pp. 24–27. Both these publications debunk the widely-held Dispensationalist interpretation of Middle East events.